BHASA'S PLAYS

A CRITICAL STUDY

BHASA'S PLAYS

A CRITICAL STUDY

EDITOR

T. GANAPATI SASTRI

GYAN

Published by

Gyan Publishing House
5, Ansari Road
Daryaganj, New Delhi-110002
Phone: 011-47034999, 9811692060
E-mail: books@gyanbooks.com

Distribution Network
gyanbooks.com
India, USA, Canada, UK, Australia

ISBN: 978-93-6780-290-8 (HB)

First Published, 1925

2nd Impression 2024

Printed at: Gyan Press, Delhi.

BHASA'S PLAYS: A CRITICAL STUDY
Editor: T. GANAPATI SASTRI

BHASA'S PLAYS

—A CRITICAL STUDY—

BY

Mahâmahopâdhyâya

T. GANAPATI SÂSTRÎ, Ph. D., M. R. A. S. (Hon.)

Trivandrum:

PRINTED AT THE SRIDHARA POWER PRESS.

1925.

NOTE.

This little volume contains a connected account of my views about Bhasa's works and a discussion of the views propounded by a few scholars, from which I differ.

CONTENTS.

—:o:—

Number	Subject		Page
1.	The acquisition of rare collection of plays	...	1
2.	The conduct of the plays ...	...	2
3.	Mutual resemblance among the plays	...	16
4.	The authorship of the plays ...	...	"
5.	Other manuscript copies discovered	...	18
6.	Enquiry as to Bhasa's age ...	...	19
7.	The merits of the works ...	...	27
8.	Bhamaha's criticism explained ...	...	33
9.	Bhasa's followers	...	35
10.	Mrichchhakatika compared ...	...	36
11.	The merits of Pratima and Svapna; Kalidasa's dependence on Bhasa	...	40
12.	Dingnaga	...	47
13.	Bhasa, a Rishi	...	48
14.	Comparison of Bhasa and Kalidasa	...	50
15.	Meeting of the contention that Kalidasa lived not long after Bhasa	...	53
16.	The similarity of Prakrit in Bhasa and Kalidasa	...	"
17.	Sanskrit had ceased to be a spoken language at the time of Kalidasa	...	55
18.	At the time of Mahabhashya Sanskrit had ceased to be a spoken language	...	56
19.	Prakrit had ceased to be a spoken dialect at the time of Kalidasa	...	57
20.	The origin of Sanskrit ...	...	58
21.	The origin of Prakrit	...	60
22.	The language of Asoka's time ...	...	61
23.	Bhasa's priority to Panini ...	...	62
24.	Publicity of Panini's Anusasana ...	...	63
25.	The popularity of the epic of Rama in fourth century B. C. ...	...	66
26.	Rama, an Avatara of Vishnu ...	...	68

Number	Subject	Page.
27.	Reference to Sramana	"
28.	Chanakya	69
29.	Bhasa's priority to the current Natyasastra	70
30.	The current Natyasastra, an enlarged form of the ancient one	71
31.	No patron of Bhasa suggested by the plays ...	72
32.	Summary of the conclusions	74
33.	Reference to Rajagriha etc., ...	75
34.	A rare information obtained from Pratima ...	76
35.	The richness and perfection of the characters	"
36.	Bhasa's tendency to write Rupakas... ...	"
37.	Want of circulation and the absence of reference to them in the anthologies ...	77
38.	The popularity of the plays in the Kerala country in ancient days	79
39.	The probability of the existence of the manuscripts of the plays of Bhasa in some corners of India	80
40.	Some contrary views and their refutation ...	"
	(a) Ramavatara Sarma	81
	(b) Bhattanatha Swami	82
	(c) Dr. L. D. Barnett	94
	(d) Messrs Krishna Pisharodi and Rama Pisharodi	96
	(e) Some other doubts regarding Bhasa's authorship; Prof. Levi, Dr. Barnett etc. ...	110
	(f) Dr. Sukthankar	122
41.	The cause that led to the discovery of the plays in Travancore, and the conclusion. ...	124
	Appendix I.	
	" II–a, b, c, d, e and f.	

BHASA'S PLAYS.

In the year 1909, when the Department for the publication of Sanskrit manuscripts was organised under my charge by the Government of His Highness the Maharaja of Travancore, I came across a palm-leaf manuscript of *Natakas* in the *Manalikkara Matham* near Padmanabhapuram. It was found to contain 105 leaves with ten lines of twenty granthas in each page written in old Malayalam characters. Though the manuscript seemed to be more than three hundred years old, there was no defacement of characters except in certain parts of the first twelve leaves. The style and dignity of conception appeared to me to be such as characterise the great works of the Rishis, and superior to what we find in famous works of the great poets. On examination, the manuscript was found to contain the following ten *Rupakas*:—

The Acquisition of a Rare Collection of Plays.

1. Svapnavasavadatta
2. Pratijnayaugandharayana
3. Pancharatra
4. Charudatta
5. Dutaghatotkacha
6. Avimaraka
7. Balacharita
8. Madhyamavyayoga
9. Karnabhara
10. Urubhanga

Besides, there was also an eleventh *Rupaka* just begun but abruptly left unfinished towards the middle of the reverse side of the first leaf. During a subsequent tour, from one Govinda Pisharodi, an astrologer of Kailasapuram, near Kaduthurutti, were obtained two *Natakas* of a similar character, named *Abhishekanataka* and *Pratimanataka*. It was subsequently discovered that the Palace Library also contained a manuscript of each of these works. All these manuscripts written in Malayalam characters were on palm-leaves, probabaly three or four centuries old. Thus were obtained twelve or rather thirteen *Rupakas*, neither seen nor heard of before.

2. The Conduct of the Plays.

It is usual in *Natakas* to begin with *Nandi* and then to state "नान्द्यन्ते सूत्रधारः". But the Natakas in this collection, as a rule begin with the stage direction 'नान्द्यन्ते ततः प्रविशति सूत्रधारः' and then the *mangala loka* is introduced. Again, instead of the word *Prastavana* these *Natakas* use the word *Sthapana*. Thirdly, in the *Natakas* of *Sudraka*, *Kalidasa* and others, in the ***Prastavana***, mention is made of the name of the author and of the works and in some instances in terms of praise. But in the plays before us, in the *Sthapana*, not even the name is brought in either of the works or of the author. In the "*Bharata Vakya*" or the closing sentence of every one of these plays, invariably occurs the prayer:—"May our greatest of kings or may our king rule the land". In all these plays there is at the close a sentence announcing such and such a *Nataka* is finished and here the name of the work is given. All these characteristic features can be made out from the following quotations which form the initial and closing portions of *Svapnanataka* and other plays. The beginning of *Svapnanataka*:—

"(नान्द्यन्ते ततः प्रविशति सूत्रधारः)

सूत्रधारः—

उदयनवेन्दुसवर्णावासवदत्ताबलौ बलस्य त्वाम् ।
पद्मावतीर्णपूर्णौ वसन्तकम्रौ भुजौ पाताम् ॥

एवमार्यमिश्रान् विज्ञापयामि । अये किन्नु खलु मयि विज्ञापनव्यग्रे शब्द इव श्रूयते । अङ्ग ! पश्यामि ।

(नेपथ्ये)

उस्सरह उस्सरह अय्या ! उस्सरह ।

सूत्रधारः— भवतु, विज्ञातम् ।

भृत्यैर्मगधराजस्य स्निग्धैः कन्यानुगामिभिः ।
धृष्टमुत्सार्यते सर्वस्तपोवनगतो जनः ॥

(निष्क्रान्तः ।)

स्थापना

The ending of *Svapnanataka*—

(भरतवाक्यम्)

इमां सागरपर्यन्तां हिमवद्विन्ध्यकुण्डलाम् ।
महीमेकातपत्राङ्कां राजसिंहः प्रशास्तु नः ॥

षष्ठोऽङ्कः ।

स्वप्ननाटकमवसितम् ।"

The beginning of *Pratijnayaugandharayana*:—

"(नान्द्यन्ते ततः प्रविशति सूत्रधारः ।)

सूत्रधारः—

पातु वासवदत्तायो महासेनोऽतिवीर्यवान् ।
वत्सराजस्तु नाम्ना सशक्तिर्यौगन्धरायणः ॥

(परिक्रम्य नेपथ्याभिमुखमवलोक्य) आर्ये ! इतस्तावत् ।

(प्रविश्य)

नटी—अय्य ! इअह्मि ।

सूत्रधारः—आर्ये ! गीयतां तावत् किञ्चिद् वस्तु । ततस्तव गीत-प्रसाधिते रङ्गे वयमपि प्रकरणमारभामहे । आर्ये ! किमिदं चिन्त्यते ननु गीयते ।

नटी—अज्ज ! मए सिविणे णादिकुळस्स अस्सत्थं विअ दिट्ठं । ता इच्छामि अय्येण कुसळविण्णाणणिमित्तं कञ्चिं पुरुसं पेक्खिदुं ।

सूत्रधारः—बाढम् ।

पुरुषं प्रेषयिष्यामि व्यक्तमात्महिते क्षमम् ।

(नेपथ्ये)

सालक! सज्जस्त्वम् ।

सूत्रधारः—

पुरुषं प्रेषयत्येष यथा यौगन्धरायणः ॥

(निष्क्रान्तौ ।)

स्थापना

The ending of *Paratijnayaugandharayana*:—

"(भरतवाक्यम्)

भवन्त्वरजसो गावः परचक्रं प्रशाम्यतु ।
इमामपि महीं कृत्स्नां राजसिंहः प्रशास्तु नः ॥

(निष्क्रान्ताः सर्वे ।)

चतुर्थोऽङ्कः ।

प्रतिज्ञानाटिकावसिता ॥"

The beginning of *Pancharatra*:—

"(नान्द्यन्ते ततः प्रविशति सूत्रधारः ।)

सूत्रधारः—

द्रोणः पृथिव्यर्जुनभीमदूतो यः कर्णधारः शकुनीश्वरस्य ।
दुर्योधनो भीमयुधिष्ठिरः स पायाद् विराडुत्तरगोऽभिमन्युः ॥

(परिक्रम्य) एवमार्यमिश्रान् विज्ञापयामि । अये किन्नुखलु मयि विज्ञापनव्यग्रे शब्द इव श्रूयते । अङ्ग! पश्यामि ।

(नेपथ्ये)

अहो कुरुराजस्य यज्ञसमृद्धिः ।

सूत्रधारः —भवतु, विज्ञातम् ।

सर्वैरन्तःपुरैः सार्धं प्रीत्या प्राप्तेषु राजसु ।
यज्ञो दुर्योधनस्यैष कुरुराजस्य वर्तते ॥

(निष्क्रान्तः ।)

स्थापना ।"

—The ending of *Pancharatra*:—

"**द्रोणः** —

इत्यर्थं वयमानीताः पञ्चरात्रोऽपि वर्तते ।
धर्मेणावर्जिता भिक्षा धर्मेणैव प्रदीयताम् ॥

दुर्योधनः —

बाढं दत्तं मया राज्यं पाण्डवेभ्यो यथापुरम् ।
मृतेऽपि हि नराः सर्वे सत्ये तिष्ठन्ति तिष्ठति ॥

द्रोणः —

हन्त सर्वे प्रसन्नाः स्मः प्रवृद्धकुलसंग्रहाः ।
इमामपि महीं कृत्स्नां राजसिंहः प्रशास्तु नः ॥

(निष्क्रान्ताः सर्वे ।)

तृतीयोऽङ्कः ॥

अवसितं पञ्चरात्रम् ।"

The beginning of *Charudatta*:—

"(नान्द्यन्ते ततः प्रविशति सूत्रधारः ।)

सूत्रधारः —किण्णुहु अज्ज पच्चूस एव्व निक्खन्तस्स बुभुक्खाए पुक्खरपत्तपडिदजळबिन्दू विअ चञ्चळाअन्ति विअ मे अक्खीणि । (परि-

क्रम्य) जाव गेहं गच्छिअ जाणामि किण्णुहु संविधा विहिदा ण वेत्तिं। एदं अह्माणं गेहं । जाव पविशामि । (प्रविश्यावलोक्य) जह ळोहीपरिक्ट्ठणकालसारा भूमी णेउब्भामणसुगन्धो विअ गन्धो सुणिमित्तं विअ परिब्भमन्तो वडिवस्सअजणो। किण्णु खु संविधा विहिदा । आदु बुभुक्खाए ओदणमअं विअ जीवळोअं पेक्खामि । अय्ये! इदो दाव ।

नटी — अय्य! इअह्मि । अय्य! दिट्ठिआ खु सि आअदो ।

सूत्रधारः—अय्ये! किं अत्थि अह्माणं गेहे कोवि पादरासो ।

नटी — अत्थि ।

सूत्रधारः — चिरं जीव । एवं सोहणाणि दत्तिआ होहि ।

....

सूत्रधारः — कहिण्णु खु दरिद्दबह्मणं ळभेअं । (विलोक्य) एसो अय्यचारुदत्तस्स वअस्सो अय्यमेत्तेयो णाम बह्मणो इदो एव्व आअच्छदि । जाव उवणिमन्तेमि । (परिक्रम्य) अय्य! णिमन्तिदो सि । आमन्तणस्स मा दरिद्दत्ति अवमण्णेहि । संपण्णं अह्णिदव्वं भविस्सदि । घिदं गुळं दहिं तण्डुला अ सव्वं अत्थि। अविअ दक्खिणामासआणि भविस्सन्ति ।

(नेपथ्ये)

अण्णं अण्णं णिमन्तेदु दाव भवं । अरित्तओ दाव अहं ।

सूत्रधारः —

घिदगुळदहिसुसमिद्धं धूविअसूवोवदंससंभिण्णं ।
सक्कारदत्तमिट्ठं भुञ्जीयदु भत्तमय्येण ॥

(निष्क्रान्तः ।)

स्थापना ।"

The ending of *Charudatta*: —

गणिका — एहि इमं अळङ्कारं गह्णिअ अय्यचारुदत्तं अहिसरिस्सामो ।

चेटी — अज्जुए ! तह । एदं पुण अभिसारिआसहायभूदं दुद्दिणं उण्णमिदं ।

गणिका — हदासे ! मा खु वड्ढावेहि ।

चेटी — एदु एदु अज्जुआ ।

(इति निष्क्रान्ते ।)

चतुर्थोऽङ्कः ॥

अवसितं चारुदत्तम् ।"

The beginning of *Dutaghatotkacha*:—

"(नान्द्यन्ते ततः प्रविशति सूत्रधारः ।)

सूत्रधारः —

नारायणस्त्रिभुवनैकपरायणो वः पायादुपायगतयुक्तिकरः सुराणाम् ।
लोकत्रयाविरतनाटकतन्त्रवस्तुप्रस्तावनप्रतिसमापनसूत्रधारः ॥

एवमार्यमिश्रान् विज्ञापयामि । अये किन्नुखलु मयि विज्ञापनव्यग्रे शब्द इव श्रूयते । अङ्ग ! पश्यामि ।

(नेपथ्ये)

भो ! भोः ! निवेद्यतां निवेद्यतां तावत् ।

सूत्रधारः — भवतु, विज्ञातम् । एष खलु संशप्तकानीकनिवाहिते जनार्दनसहाये धनञ्जये तदनन्तरमुपगतभीष्मवधामर्षितैर्धार्तराष्ट्रैः परिवार्य निहतः कुमारोऽभिमन्युः । तथाहि —

यान्त्यर्जुनप्रत्यभियानभीता यतोऽर्जुनस्तां दिशमीक्षमाणाः ।
नराधिपाः स्वानि निवेशनानि सौभद्रबाणाङ्कितनष्टसंज्ञाः ॥

(निष्क्रान्तः ।)

स्थापना ।"

The ending of *Dutaghatotkacha.*—

"घटोत्कचः —भो भो राजानः! श्रूयतां जनार्दनस्य पश्चिमसन्देशः,
धर्मं समाचर कुरु स्वजनव्यपेक्षां यत् काङ्क्षितं मनसि सर्वमिहानुतिष्ठ।
जात्योपदेश इव पाण्डवरूपधारी सूर्यांशुभिः सममुपैष्यति वः कृतान्तः॥

(इति निष्क्रान्ताः सर्वे।)

दूतघटोत्कचमवसितम्॥"

The beginning of *Avimaraka*:—

"(नान्द्यन्ते ततः प्रविशति सूत्रधारः।)

सूत्रधारः —

उत्क्षिप्तां सानुकम्पं सलिलनिधिजलादेकदंष्ट्राग्ररूढा-
माक्रान्तामाजिमध्ये निहतदितिसुतामेकपादावधूताम्।
सम्भुक्तां प्रीतिपूर्वं स्वभुजवशगतामेकचक्राभिगुप्तां
श्रीमान् नारायणस्त्वे प्रदिशतु वसुधामुच्छ्रितैकातपत्राम्॥

नेपथ्याभिमुखमवलोक्य) आर्ये! इतस्तावत्।

(प्रविश्य)

नटी —अय्य! इअह्मि।

सूत्रधारः —आर्ये! तव वदनजनितकौतूहलेन स्मितेन निवेदित इवान्तर्गतो भावः। ननु किञ्चिद् वक्तुकामासि।

नटी —को एत्थ विह्मओ, अय्यो भावण्णो त्ति।

सूत्रधारः — तेन हि स्वैरमभिधीयताम्।

नटी —इच्छेमि अय्येण सह उय्याणं गन्तुं। अत्थि मे तहिं इत्थि-आकरणीअं णिअमकय्यं।

(नेपथ्ये)

भूतिक! त्वमप्युद्यानं गच्छ कुरङ्गीरक्षणार्थं, मदावस्थो ह्यञ्जन-गिरिः।

सूत्रधारः — आर्ये! ननु भवत्या श्रुतम् — उद्यानं गता राजपुत्रीति। तस्मात् सम्प्रति सर्वतः परिगुप्तानि भवन्त्युद्यानानि । प्रतिनिवृत्तायां राजसुतायां स्वैरं गमिष्यावः ।

नटी — जं अय्यो आणवेदि ।

(निष्क्रान्तौ ।)

स्थापना ।"

The ending of *Avimaraka*:—

(भरतवाक्यम्)

भवन्त्वरजसो गावः परचक्रं प्रशाम्यतु ।
इमामपि महीं कृत्स्नां राजसिंहः प्रशास्तु नः ॥

(निष्क्रान्ताः सर्वे ।)

षष्ठोऽङ्कः ।

अविमारकस्य षष्ठोऽङ्कः । एषोऽवसितश्च ।"

The beginning of *Balacharita*:—

(नान्द्यन्ते ततः प्रविशति सूत्रधारः ।)

सूत्रधारः —

शङ्खक्षीरवपुः पुरा कृतयुगे नाम्ना तु नारायण-
स्त्रेतायां त्रिपदार्पितत्रिभुवनो विष्णुः सुवर्णप्रभः ।
दूर्वाश्यामनिभः स रावणवधे रामो युगे द्वापरे
नित्यं योऽञ्जनसन्निभः कलियुगे वः पातु दामोदरः ॥

एवमार्यमिश्रान् विज्ञापयामि । अये किन्नुखलु मयि विज्ञापनव्यग्रे शब्द इव श्रूयते । अङ्ग! पश्यामि ।

(नेपथ्ये)

अहं गगनसञ्चारी ।

सूत्रधारः —भवतु, विज्ञातम् ।

पतत्यसौ पुष्पमयी च वृष्टिर्नदन्ति तूर्याणि च देवतानाम् ।
द्रष्टुं हरिं वृष्णिकुले प्रसूतमभ्यागतो नारद एष तूर्णम् ॥

(निष्क्रान्तः ।)

The ending of *Balacharita*:—

(भरतवाक्यम्)

इमां सागरपर्यन्तां हिमवद्विन्ध्यकुण्डलाम् ।
महीमेकातपत्राङ्कां राजसिंहः प्रशास्तु नः ॥

पञ्चमोऽङ्कः ॥

अवसितं बालचरितम् ।"

The beginning of *Madhyamavyayoga*:—

(ततः प्रविशति सूत्रधारः ।)

सूत्रधारः —

पायात् स वोऽसुरवधूहृदयावसादः
पादो हरेः कुवलयामलखड्गनीलः ।
यः प्रोद्यतस्त्रिभुवनैकमणे रराज
वैदूर्यसंक्रम इवाम्बरसागरस्य ॥

एवमार्यमिश्रान् विज्ञापयामि । अये किन्नुखलु मयि विज्ञापनव्यग्रे शब्द इव श्रूयते । अङ्ग! पश्यामि ।

(नेपथ्ये)

भोस्तात! कोनुखल्वेषः ।

सूत्रधारः — भवतु, विज्ञातम् ।

भोश्शब्दोच्चारणादस्य ब्राह्मणोऽयं न संशयः ।
त्रास्यते निर्विशङ्केन केनचित् पापचेतसा ॥

(नेपथ्ये)

भोस्तात! कोनुखल्वेषः ।

सूत्रधारः—हन्त इदं विज्ञातम् । एष खलु पाण्डवमध्यमस्यात्मजो हिडिम्बारणिसम्भूतो राक्षसाग्निरकृतवैरं ब्राह्मणजनं वित्रासयति । भोः! कष्टं कष्टं खलु पत्नीसुतपरिवृतस्य ब्राह्मणस्य वृत्तान्तः । अत्र हि ।

श्रान्तैः सुतैः परिवृतस्तरुणैः सदारो वृद्धो द्विजो निशिचरानुचरः स एषः ।
व्याघ्रानुसारचरितो वृषभः सधेनुः संत्रस्तवत्सक इवा कुलतामुपैति ॥

(निष्क्रान्तः ।)

स्थापना ।

The ending of *Madhyamavyayoga*:—

"**भीमसेनः**—हिडिम्बे! इतस्तावत् । वत्स! घटोत्कच! इतस्तावत् । तत्रभवन्तं केशवदासमाश्रमपदद्वारमात्रमपि संभावयिष्यामः ।

यथा नदीनां प्रभवः समुद्रो यथाहुतीनां प्रभवो हुताशः ।
यथेन्द्रियाणां प्रभवं मनोऽपि तथा प्रभुर्नो भगवानुपेन्द्रः ॥

(निष्क्रान्ताः सर्वे ।)

मध्यमव्यायोगोऽवसितः ॥"

The beginning of *Karnabhara*:—

"(नान्द्यन्ते ततः प्रविशति सूत्रधारः)

सूत्रधारः—

नरमृगपतिवर्ष्मालोकनभ्रान्तनारी-
नरदनुजसुपर्वव्रातपातालकोकः ।
करजकुलिशपालीभिन्नदैत्येन्द्रवक्षाः
सुररिपुबलहन्ता श्रीधरोऽस्तु श्रियै वः ॥

एवमार्यमिश्रान् विज्ञापयामि । अये किन्नुखलु मयि विज्ञापनव्यग्रे शब्द इव श्रूयते । अङ्ग! पश्यामि ।

(नेपथ्ये)

भो भो! निवेद्यतां महाराजायाङ्गेश्वराय ।

सूत्रधारः — भवतु, विज्ञातम् ।

सङ्ग्रामे तुमुले जाते कर्णाय कलिताञ्जलिः ।
निवेदयति संभ्रान्तो भृत्यो दुर्योधनाज्ञया ॥

(निष्क्रान्तः ।)

प्रस्तावना ॥

The ending of *Karnabhara*:—

"(भरतवाक्यम्)

सर्वत्र सम्पदः सन्तु नश्यन्तु विपदः सदा ।
राजा राजगुणोपेतो भूमिमेकः प्रशास्तु नः ॥

(निष्क्रान्तौ)

कर्णभारमवसितम् ॥"

The beginning of *Urubhanga*:—

(नान्द्यन्ते ततः प्रविशति सूत्रधारः)

सूत्रधारः —

भीष्मद्रोणतटां जयद्रथजलां गान्धारराजह्रदां
कर्णद्रौणिकृपोर्मिनक्रमकरां दुर्योधनस्रोतसम् ।
तीर्णः शत्रुनदीं शरासिकतां येन प्लवेनार्जुनः
शत्रूणां तरणेषु वः स भगवानस्तु प्लवः केशवः ॥

एवमार्यमिश्रान् विज्ञापयामि । अये किन्नुखलु मयि विज्ञापनव्यग्रे शब्द इव श्रूयते । अङ्ग! पश्यामि ।

(नेपथ्ये)

एते स्मो भो! एते स्मः ।

सूत्रधारः — भवतु विज्ञातम् ।

(प्रविश्य)

पारिपार्श्विकः — भाव!

एतद्रणाहतगजाश्वनरेन्द्रयौधं सङ्कीर्णलेख्यमिव चित्रपटं प्रविद्धम् ।
युद्धे सुयोधनवृकोदरयोः प्रवृत्ते यौधा नरेन्द्रनिधनैकगृहं प्रविष्टाः ॥

(निष्क्रान्तौ ।)

स्थापना ॥

The ending of *Urubhanga*:—

बलदेवः —

याम्येष सज्जनघनानि तपोवनानि

धृतराष्ट्रः —

पुत्रप्रणाशविफलं हि धिगस्तु राज्यम् ।

अश्वत्थामा —

यातोऽद्य सौप्तिकवधोद्यतबाणपाणि-
र्गां पातु नो नरपतिः शमितारिपक्षः ॥

(निष्क्रान्ताः सर्वे)

ऊरुभङ्गमवसितम् ॥"

The beginning of the nameless *Nataka*:—

(नान्द्यन्ते ततः प्रविशति सूत्रधारः ।)

सूत्रधारः —

पादः पायादुपेन्द्रस्य सर्वलोकोत्सवः सवः ।
व्याविद्धो नमुचिर्येन तनुताम्रनखेन खे ॥

एवमार्यमिश्रान् विज्ञापयामि । किन्तु खलु मयि विज्ञापनव्यग्रे शब्द इव श्रूयते । अङ्ग! पश्यामि ।

(नेपथ्ये)

भो भोः प्रतिहाराधिकृताः! महाराजो दुर्योधनः समाज्ञापयति।

सूत्रधारः —भवतु, विज्ञातम्।

उत्पन्ने धार्तराष्ट्राणां विरोधे पाण्डवैः सह।
पर्येति मन्त्रशालायां भृत्यो दुर्योधनाज्ञया॥

(निष्क्रान्तः।)

स्थापना॥"

The beginning of *Abhishekanataka*:—

(नान्द्यन्ते ततः प्रविशति सूत्रधारः।)

सूत्रधारः —

यो गाधिपुत्रमखविघ्नकराभिहन्ता युद्धे विराधखरदूषणवीर्यहन्ता।
दर्पोद्धतोल्बणकबन्धकपीन्द्रहन्ता पायात् स वो निशिचरेन्द्रकुलाभिहन्ता॥

एवमार्यमिश्रान् विज्ञापयामि। (परिक्रम्यावलोक्य) अये किन्नु खलु मयि विज्ञापनव्यग्रे शब्द इव श्रूयते। अङ्ग! पश्यामि।

(नेपथ्ये)

सुग्रीव! इत इतः। ....

स्थापना॥

The ending of *Abhishekanataka*:—

(भरतवाक्यम्)

भवन्त्वरजसो गावः परचक्रं प्रशाम्यतु।
इमामपि महीं कृत्स्नां राजसिंहः प्रशास्तु नः॥

(निष्क्रान्ताः सर्वे।)

सप्तमोऽङ्कः॥

अभिषेकनाटकं समाप्तम्॥"

The beginning of *Pratimanataka*:—

(नान्द्यन्ते ततः प्रविशति सूत्रधारः ।)

सूत्रधारः —

सीताभवः पातु सुमन्त्रतुष्टः सुग्रीवरामः सहलक्ष्मणश्च ।
यो रावणार्यप्रतिमश्च देव्या विभीषणात्मा भरतोऽन्यसर्गम् ॥

(नेपथ्याभिमुखमवलोक्य) आर्ये ! इतस्तावत् ।

(प्रविश्य)

नटी — अय्य ! इअह्मि ।

सूत्रधारः — आर्ये ! इममेवेदानीं शरत्कालमधिकृत्य गीयतां तावत् ।

नटी — अय्य ! तह । (गायति ।)

सूत्रधारः — अस्मिन् हि काले,

चरति पुलिनेषु हंसी काशांशुकवासिनी सुसंहृष्टा ।

(नेपथ्ये)

अय्य ! अय्य !

सूत्रधारः — भवतु, विज्ञातम् ।

मुदिता नरेन्द्रभवने त्वरिता प्रतिहाररक्षीव ॥

(निष्क्रान्तौ ।)

स्थापना ॥

The ending of *Pratimanataka*:—

(भरतवाक्यम्)

यथा रामश्च जानक्या बन्धुभिश्च समागतः ।
तथा लक्ष्म्या समायुक्तो राजा भूमिं प्रशास्तु नः ॥

(निष्क्रान्ताः सर्वे ।)

सप्तमोऽङ्कः ॥

प्रतिमानाटकं समाप्तम् ॥"

Besides exhibiting a structural similarity, these plays also contain, as the above quotations will show, several passages in common, e g. "एवमार्यमिश्रान् विज्ञापयामि । अये किन्नु खलु मयि विज्ञापनव्यग्रे शब्द इव श्रूयते । अङ्ग ! पश्यामि ।" is found in all plays except *Pratijna*, *Charudatta*, *Avimaraka*, *Pratima* and *Karnabhara*. Again the sloka—

3. Mutual resemblance among the plays.

"इमां सागरपर्यन्तां हिमवद्विन्ध्यकुण्डलाम् ।
महीमेकातपत्राङ्कां राजसिंहः प्रशास्तु नः ॥"

appears as the *Bharata Vakya* both in *Svapnavasavadatta* and in *Balacharita*. The passage—

"भवन्त्वरजसो गावः परचक्रं प्रशाम्यतु ।
इमामपि महीं कृत्स्नां राजसिंहः प्रशास्तु नः ॥"

is seen in the plays *Pratijna*, *Avimaraka* and *Abhisheka* and the latter half of the sloka occurs in *Pancharatra* also. The practice of suggesting names of the principal *Dramatis Personae* in the benedictory verse is alike in *Pratijna*, *Pancharatra*, *Pratima* and *Svapnanataka*. The sloka—

"लिम्पतीव तमोऽङ्गानि वर्षतीवाञ्जनं नभः ।
असत्पुरुषसेवेव दृष्टिर्निष्फलतां गता ॥"

appears in the first Act of both *Charudatta* and *Balacharita*. The passage "किं वक्ष्यतीति हृदयं परिशङ्कितमे" occurs in the sixth Act of *Svapnanataka* and also in the fourth act of *Abhishekanataka*. The part "धर्मस्नेहान्तरेन्यस्ता" of a sloka is seen in both the second act of *Pratima* and in the sixth act of *Abhishekanataka*. Many more points of similarity of this kind can be observed in the plays.

As indicated by these points of close similarity, it is very likely that all these plays are the work of the same author. As neither the name of the author nor that of the work is mentioned in the *Sthapana* of these plays, it seems to me that they must have been written before such a practice came into vogue. Having regard to the various poetic excellences which will be

4. The authorship of the plays.

hereafter noticed, I should think that the author was a great poet of antiquity and of wide renown. What we have till now known as *Svapnavasavadatta*, though only in name, from ancient works of such great authors as *Acharyabhinavagupta-pada* and others, may in all probability be the same work as this *Svapnanataka*, which is perhaps only a contracted form of the full name; for, in *Svapnanataka*, we have the description of the prince *Vatsaraja's* dream about *Vasavadatta*. These considerations make me regard this series of plays with unusual appreciation, for it is well-known that *Svapnavasavadatta* which was till now thought to have been lost for ever was composed by the great poet *Bhasa* as the following sloka of *Rajasekhara* in *Suktimuktavali* shows: —

"भासनाटकचक्रेऽपिच्छेकैः क्षिप्ते परीक्षितुम् ।
स्वप्नवासवदत्तस्य दाहकोऽभून्न पावकः ॥"

This great poet it is who is enshrined in the passage in the *Prastavana* of *Malavikagnimitra* by *Kalidasa* "प्रथितयशसां भाससौमिल्लकविपुत्रादीनां प्रबन्धानतिक्रम्य" and in the following sloka by *Bhatta Bana* in *Harshacharita*.

"सूत्रधारकृतारम्भैर्नाटकैर्बहुभूमिकैः ।
सपताकैर्यशो लेभे भासो देवकुलैरिव ॥"

I am surprised to find that a few have been labouring under an erroneous impression that *Bhasa* and *Dhavaka* are identical. *Bhasa* is described by *Kalidasa* as a very ancient poet in his *Malavikagnimitra*, while *Dhavaka* was only a contemporary and protege of *Harsha*, the author of *Ratnavali*, as is evident from the well-known line "श्रीहर्षादेर्धावकादीनामिव धनम्" in the *Kavyaprakasa* as well as from the comments thereon "धावको रत्नावलीनाटिकाप्रणयनसहायः" in the *Kavyaprakasa-Brihattika* by *Sri Vidyachakravartin*. How can these two poets who flourished in different centuries be deemed identical? †

These *Natakas* being thus seen to be the works of *Bhasa*, the epithet 'सूत्रधारकृतारम्भैः' by which *Bhatta Bana* in the above

† Vide appendix II (a)

sloka qualifies *Bhasa's Natakas*, may apply to these plays, for every one of them begins with the stage direction "नान्द्यन्ते ततः ततः प्रविशति सूत्रधारः"

5. Other manuscript copies discovered.

As the manuscript of *Svapnavasavadatta*, the best known of the series, was moth-eaten in several places, and the manuscripts of *Karnabhara* and *Charudatta* were incomplete, I tried to obtain complete manuscripts of these plays, with a view to edit and publish them. With this end in view, I addressed several Sanskrit scholars, European as well as Indian. Many of them replied to say that even these manuscripts, however incomplete, of *Bhasa's Natakas* which had long been regarded as lost, were in themselves a very great acquisition; but fortunately, I was able to obtain a complete, though not correct, manuscript of each of the two plays *Pratijna* and *Svapnavasavadata*, This was from my friend Pandit A. Anantacharya of Mysore who was kind enough to send me a copy of his copy of the manscript he had obtained from Kerala. At the end of this manuscript copy of *Svapnavasavadatta* is written "स्वप्नवासवदत्ता समाप्ता." This agrees with what we supposed to be the full name of *Svapnanataka*. At the end of the manuscript of *Pratijnanatika* is written the full name of *Pratijna-yaugandharayana*. After this, during another tour, I obtained at Haripad a manuscript of *Avimaraka* from Mr. Subramonyan Moottatu of Puttiyal. The *Svapnavasavadatta* with the aid of the new manuscript has assumed a complete form and I feel fully rewarded for my pains on this account. When *Svapnavasavadatta* was just in the press another manuscript of it was secured from Krishnan Tantri of Thazhamon Matham in *Chengannur* and separate manuscript of *Pratijnayaugandharayana* and of *Abhishekanataka* were also obtained from the same source.

After *Svapnavasavadatta* and some other plays were published, a manuscript of the *Svapna* was obtained from the Kilimanur Palace and another manuscript with a number of plays other than *Svapnavasavadatta*, from Mr. Nilakanthan Chakyar of Manganam. Also a complete copy of the fragmentary play already referred to as not revealing its name was then found to exist in the codex secured from Mr. Subramonyan Moottatu of Puttiyal; and its name was learnt to be *Dutavakya* as shown by the concluding passage of the play:—

"(भरतवाक्यम्)

"इमां सागरपर्यन्तां हिमवद्विन्ध्यकुण्डलाम् ।
महीमेकातपत्राङ्कां राजसिंहः प्रशास्तु नः ॥

(निष्क्रान्ताः सर्वे ।)

दूतवाक्यं समाप्तम् ॥"

---

6. Enquiry as to Bhasa's age.

The grand and charming beauty with which things are described in exact resemblance to nature, and the choice of simple apt and felicitous words are features so peculiarly characteristic of these *Rupakas* that they outshine *Kalidasa's* and come near, in these respects, to the excellence of epic poets *Valmiki* and *Vyasa.* On this ground alone the antiquity of *Bhasa* could be well established. Other arguments are also shown in support of the theory. Doubtless it is to this *Svapnavasavadatta* of ours that *Vandyaghatiya Sarvananda* who lived about 1159 A. D. of the Christian era, refers when he, in his *Amarakosatikasarvasava* says in commenting on the sloka, "श्रृङ्गारवीरकरुणा" that "स्वादेशमात्मसात्कर्तुम् उदयनस्य पद्मावतीपारणयोऽर्थश्रृङ्गारः स्वप्नवासवदत्ते, तृतीयस्तस्यैव वासवदत्तापरिणयः कामश्रृङ्गारः". *Acharyabhinavaguptapada* who lived in the 10th century A.D. speaks of *Svapnavasavadatta* in his *Bharatanatyavedavivriti* "क्वचित् क्रीडायथा स्वप्नवासवदत्तायां" Therein another *Nataka* is also mentioned under the name of *Daridra Charudatta.* I think that it is our *Charudattanataka.*

Vamana, who flourished long before *Anandavardhana*, the author of *Dhvanyaloka* of the 9th century A. D., quotes in the third Adhyaya of the fourth Adhikarana of his *Kavyalankarasutravritti*, the following sloka which occurs in the fourth act of *Svapnavasavadatta*:-

"शरच्छशाङ्कगौरेण वाताविद्धेन भामिनि ! ।
काशपुष्पलवेनेदं साश्रुपातं मुखं मम ॥"

In the second Adhyaya of the 5th Adhikarana is also quoted the passage "यो भर्तृपिण्डस्य कृते न युध्येत्" which is the fourth pada of a certain sloka in the fourth act of *Pratijnayaugandharayana*. In the fifth Adhikarana of the same work is quoted the sloka,

"यासां बलिर्भवति मद्गृहदेहलीनां
हंसैश्च सारसगणैश्च विलुप्तपूर्वः ।
तास्वेव पूर्वबलिरूढयवाङ्कुरासु
बीजाञ्जलिः पतति कीटमुखावलीढः ॥"

which occurs in the first act of *Charudattanataka*. The former half of the sloka,

"लिम्पतीव तमोऽङ्गानि वर्षतीवाञ्जनं नभः ।
असत्पुरुषसेवेव दृष्टिर्निष्फलतां गता ॥"

which occurs in the first act of both *Balacharita* and *Charudatta*, is quoted by *Dandin* of the 6th century A. D in the second *Parichcheda* of his *Kavyadarsa*:-

"लिम्पतीव तमोऽङ्गानि वर्षतीवाञ्जनं नभः ।
इतीदमपि भूयिष्ठमुत्प्रेक्षालक्षणान्वितम् ॥"

The *Arya*,

"स्वञ्चितपक्ष्मकवाटं नयनद्वारं स्वरूपतडनेन (?) ।
उद्घाट्य सा प्रविष्टा हृदयगृहं मे नृपतनूजा ॥"

is quoted in the 3rd *Udyota* of *Dhvanyalokalochana* as being taken from *Svapnavasavadatta*. But I should think that this sloka is not from *Svapnavasavadatta*, for it is found in none of the three manuscripts of ours. Besides this sloka apparently signifies the springing up of love for a lady at first sight. It should be either for *Vasavadatta* or *Padmavati*. But it could not be for the former, for the troubled thoughts of a lover for his far-off lady appear in this *Nataka* only long after a happy wedded life; nor could it be for the latter, for, she was offered to *Vatsaraja* even without his request at a time when he was much afflicted with thoughts of *Vasavadatta*. This surely could not be the occasion for describing his love for *Padmavati*. It is thus seen that this sloka could not find a place in *Svapnavasavadatta*. Hence, we could not infer even that this was an omission in the readings of some manuscripts, owing to the *Nataka* having ceased from circulation. Again, in the explanation of the 85th *Karika* of the 6th *Parichcheda* of the *Sahityadarpana* the sloka,

"उत्साहातिशयं वत्स ! तव बाल्यं च पश्यतः ।
मम हर्षविषादाभ्यामाक्रान्तं युगपन्मनः ॥"

is quoted from *Balacharita* as occurring therein. But this sloka may very likely have been taken from a *Balacharita* relating to *Sri Rama*, for the commentator of the *Sahityadarpana*, in explaining the above sloka adds that it is addressed by *Parasu Rama* to *Sri Rama*. And so it is that this sloka is not found in our *Balacharita* which relates to *Sri Krishna*. And this *Rama Balacharita* may probably be a work of *Bhasa*. For *Abhisheka* owes its subject matter to *Kishkindha*, *Sundara* and *Yuddha Kandas* and the *Pratimanataka* takes its materials from the *Ayodhya* and *Aranya Kandas*. Thus it is not out of place to surmise that *Bhasa* in his zeal to compose dramas out of *Purva Ramayana* should have also written a *Nataka* based on the remaining *Balakanda*.

Bhamaha in the fourth chapter of his *Kavyalankara* illustrates *Nyayavirodha* as follows:-

"विजिगीषुमुपन्यस्य वत्सेशं वृद्धदर्शनम् ।
तस्यैव कृतिनः पश्चादभ्यधाच्चारशून्यताम् ॥
अन्तर्योधशताकीर्णं सालङ्कायननेतृकम् ।
तथाविधं गजच्छद्म नाज्ञासीत् स स्वभूतगतम् ॥
यदिवोपेक्षितं तस्य सचिवैः स्वार्थसिद्धये ।
अहोनु मन्दिमा तेषां भक्तिर्वा नास्ति भर्तरि ॥
शरा दृढधनुर्मुक्ता मन्युमद्भिररातिभिः ।
मर्माणि परिहृत्यास्य पतिष्यन्तीति का नुमा ॥

हतोऽनेन मम भ्राता मम पुत्रः पिता मम ।
मातुलो भागिनेयश्च रुषा संरब्धचेतसः ॥

अस्यन्तो विविधान्याजावायुधान्यपराधिनम् ।
एकाकिनमरण्यान्यां न हन्युर्बहवः कथम् ॥

नमोऽस्तु तेभ्यो विद्वद्भ्यो येऽभिप्रायं कवेरिमम् ।
शास्त्रलोकावपास्यैव नयन्ति नयवेदिनः ॥

सचेतसो वनेभस्य चर्मणा निर्मितस्य च ।
विशेषं वेद बालोऽपि कष्टं किन्नु कथंनु तत् ॥

The subject reviewed by *Bhamaha* above,is seen in its entirety in *Pratijnanatika*. Moreover, the Prakrit passage "अणेण मम भादा हदो, अणेण मम पिदा, अणेण मम सुदो"in the first act of *Pratijnanatika* is quoted in the form of verse "हतोऽनेन मम भ्राता मम पुत्रः पिता मम" by *Bhamaha* in his enquiry on *Nyayavirodha*. The name itself of the *Natika* is not mentioned by *Bhamaha*, probabaly on account of the *Natika* having been well-known in his days. The subject of *Bhamaha's* enquiry is found in the *Brihatkatha* also. This should not lead one to infer that *Bhamaha* had *Brihatkatha* in view, and not *Pratijnanatika*, for the passage "हतोऽनेन मम भ्राता" quoted by *Bhamaha* occurs in *Pratijna*, while nothing authorises to infer that the same passage occurs in *Brihatkatha*. The fact, however, is, as we will show presently, *Brihatkatha* was written only after the age of *Bhamaha*. *Bhahmacharya*, it seems to me, must have lived long prior to *Kalidasa*. For, while he mentions such names of poets and poems as *Medhavi*, *Ramasarma*, *Asmakavamsa*, *Ratnaharana*, *Achyutottara*, all unknown to us, he has never mentioned the name of *Kalidasa* of world-wide fame or any of his works of supreme excellence. But had *Bhamaha* ever seen the poems of *Kalidasa* he would have of course mentioned them or made them also, as in the case of *Pratijnanatika*, subject to his criticism. *Bhamaha* in his "युक्तायुक्त-विचार" (enquiry into poetic conceits) speaks of the fashion of making messengers of clouds, wind etc.

"अयुक्तिमद् यथा दूता जलभृन्मारुतादयः ।
तथा भ्रमरहारीतचक्रवाकशुकादयः ॥

अवाचोऽव्यक्तवाचश्च दूरदेशविचारिणः ।
कथं दूत्यं प्रपद्येरन्निति युक्तया न युज्यते ॥

यदि चोत्कण्ठया तत्तदुन्मत्त इव भाषते ।
तथा भवतु भूम्नेदं सुमेधोभिः प्रयुज्यते ॥

(*Bhamaha's Kavyalankara, Parichcheda I*)

From this, we cannot conclude that *Bhamaha* was conversant with the poem, *Meghaduta*, for then we could as well infer that he knew also of *Sukasandesa* written by a poet of yesterday. Hence I think that by these slokas, our *Acharya* only teaches us generally that the fashion in some of our *Kavyas* of lovers sending messages through such inanimate objects as the wind, the moon, the clouds and such living inarticulate creatures as the bee, the *Chakravaka* and the parrot is not desirable on the occasions when the sender of the messages is in a state of sobriety. Bearing in mind this instruction of our *Acharya, Kalidasa*, with his keen sense of poetic propriety, observes, in defence of his message through the clouds, at the beginning of *Meghaduta*:-

"धूमज्योतिःसलिलमरुतां सन्निपातः क्व मेघः
संदेशार्थाः क्व पटुकरणैः प्राणिभिः प्रापणीयाः ।
इत्यौत्सुक्यादपरिगणयन् गुह्यकस्तं ययाचे
कामार्ता हि प्रकृतिकृपणाश्चेतनाचेतनेषु ॥"

Thus it is seen that *Bhamaha* lived much prior to *Kalidasa*. Again in the passage, "प्राप्यावन्तीनुदयनकथाकोविदग्रामवृद्धान्" of *Meghaduta*, *Kalidasa* speaks of the aged villagers of *Avanti*, clever in relating the story of *Udayana*. This may lead one to believe that the old villagers of *Avanti* at the time of of *Kalidasa* might have seen *Udayana* in their younger days and that *Udayana's* age must be only a little earlier than *Kalidasa's*. If so, how can *Bhamaha's* priority to *Kalidasa* hold good, seeing that *Bhamaha* does not even hint at

Vatsaraja's proximity in time, but speaks of him as a character of remote history or romance? But this is not so, for, in the *Prastavana* of *Malavikagnimitra*, *Kalidasa* speaks of *Bhasa* of wide spread fame "प्रथितयशसां भाससौमिल्लकविपुत्रादीनां प्रबन्धानतिक्रम्य वर्तमानकवेः कालिदासस्य क्रियायां कथं बहुमानः" and h regards the works of *Bhasa* as belonging to a very ancient date, "पुराणमित्येव न साधु सर्वं न चापि काव्यं नवमित्यवद्यम्." This means that in the course of a long period, *Bhasa's* fame had been gradually growing until in *Kalidasa's* time it reached its summit; and several centuries should have intervened between *Bhasa* and *Kalidasa* to justify such language. It is certain therefore that *Bhasa* is anterior to *Kalidasa* and *Udayana* is still farther removed from him. Hence, *Udayana*, the hero of *Bhasa's Nataka*, has not the slightest chance of being placed a little before *Kalidasa*. The passage "उदयनकथाकोविदग्रामवृद्धान्" means really this: that the old villagers having heard of the ancient romantic story of *Udayana* of their own village are fond of telling the wonderful tale, as all old men are; and not that they have seen *Udayana*. Thus *Bhamaha's* long priority to *Kalidasa* is confirmed. Again, *Bhamaha* in discussing in his *Kavyalankara*, the form of a *Katha* and an *Akhyayika*, does not mention *Brihatkatha*, which, from the peculiarity of the *Katha*, deserves mention in that connection and to which *Dandin* under the same topic in his *Kavadarsa* refers,

"भूतभाषामयीं प्राहुरद्भुतार्थां बृहत्कथाम् ।"

I should therefore conclude that, at the time of *Bhamaha*, *Brihatkatha* had not come into existence. Only after *Bhamaha's* time, those wonderful and interesting stories were culled from the *Itihasas*, from *Svapnavasavadatta* and other *Kavyas* and from folk-lore and woven by *Gunadhya* with additions of his own into that treasure house of stories called *Brihatkatha*. *Gunadhya's* was a contemporary of *Salivahana* the founder of the era of that name. *Bhamaha's* date being thus earlier than *Gunadhya* goes back to the first century preceding the Christian era. The author of our *Natakas* deserving of course a date much earlier than that of *Bhamaha* must necessarily be placed not later than the third or the second century B. C.

Again, *Vishnugupta* (alias *Chanakya* or *Kautalya*) the great propounder of politics, a contemporary of *Chandragupta Maurya* is known to have lived in the fourth century B. C. In his *Kautaliya Arthasastra* where he tells us how, on the eve of war, ministers and priests shoud breathe spirit and enthusiasm into soldiers, he observes:—

"'तुल्यवेतनोऽस्मि भवद्भिः सहभोग्यमिदं राज्यं, मयाभिहितः परोऽभिहन्तव्यः' इति, वेदेष्वप्यनुश्रूयते समाप्तदक्षिणानां यज्ञानामवभृथेषु—'सा ते गतिर्या शूराणाम्' इति, अपीह श्लोकौ भवतः—

यान् यज्ञसङ्घैस्तपसा च विप्राः स्वर्गैषिणः पात्रचयैश्च यान्ति ।
क्षणेन तानप्यति यान्ति शूराः प्राणान् सुयुद्धेषु परित्यजन्तः ॥
नवं शरावं सलिलैः सुपूर्णं सुसंस्कृतं दर्भकृतोत्तरीयम् ।
तत् तस्य माभून्नरकं च गच्छेद् यो भर्तृपिण्डस्य कृते न युध्येत् ॥

इति मन्त्रिपुरोहिताभ्यामुत्साहयेद् योधान् ।"

(*Kautalya's Arthasastra*, Adhikarana 10, Adhyaya 3)

The substance of the passage is: that to the brave is reserved a happy end, those who lose their life in battle attain that which is won by long penance and sacrifices. The victorious are ever honoured on earth but he who shrinks from fighting for the royal master by whom he is fed is a sinner destined for hell. This sloka "नवं शरावं" which is quoted above is found in the fourth act of *Pratijnayaugandharayana* addressed to soldiers to stimulate them to fight. Now we have to see whether this sloka is borrowed from the *Nataka* by the author of *Arthasastra* or the other way. When a minister out of policy addresses soldiers on the nobility of death in battle and the sinfulness of shrinking from fighting in the cause of one's master, his words are not likely to be credited, unless backed by authority. Hence the first quotation "सा ते गतिर्या शूराणां" from the sacred *Sruti*. This is followed by two slokas which read as cited from a source which, in importance, is of equal force with the *Smritis*. Hence the sloka

"नवं शरावं" could not be the words of the author of *Arthasastra* Further the fact that it immediately follows another quotation also proves it to be a quotation. For, the previous sloka "यान् यज्ञसङ्घैः" is obviously a quotation as the word to which both 'यान्' and 'तान्' refer is not in the sloka, but has to be gathered, as shown by the construction, from the passage preceding it in the work from which it is quoted. And this verse has, in fact, been traced in *Parasara Smriti*. Again, *Kautalya* introduces the two slokas with "अपीह श्लोकौ भवतः" (meaning, 'here are the slokas on the subject') which he never does in cases of his own slokas. But on two occasions *Kautalya* quotes verses of his own with this remark "Here, there is this," once in Adhikarana VII, Adhyaya VI in the *Samhita Prayanika Prakarana*; and again in Adhikarana VII, Adhyaya IX in the *Hiranya Sandhi Prakarana*. But such is not the case. "Here, there is this" shows that what follows is in completion of what was said before with which it forms a part; and that it does not purport to strengthen what has already been concluded, because the stanzas quoted do not profess to establish anything that has been said before; and also because the quotation is not specifically stated to be "Slokas" when the author says "Here, there is also this" and not "Here, there are these stanzas." Such a statement has significance only as referring to a quotation. Moreover there is also this that *Vamana* in his *Kavyalankara* in examining in the *Prayogikadhikarana* the appropriateness and correctness of the various forms and expressions found in poetry, quotes the last '*Pada*' of this stanza and examines the correctness of 'युध्येत्' found in that *Pada*. So *Vamana* regards this verse as belonging to the domain of literature and *Pratijna* is the only known work of literature where this verse is found and that decides that *Bhasa* must be its author. Further in *Kavyas*, the authors having an easy and graceful command over words express their ideas, scientific or popular, naturally in their own words. But if ever they quote from others' works they do so with an unmistakable indication. As there is no such indication in *Pratijnayaugandharayana*, in the case of the sloka 'नवं शरावं' I should think it is *Bhasa*'s own sloka quoted by *Chanakya*, the author of the *Arthasastra*. Thus we see our *Bhasa's* priority to *Chanakya*.

In the fifth act of *Pratimanataka*, in the passage addressed to *Rama* by *Ravana*, one *Medhatithi* is mentioned, "भोः काश्यपगोत्रोऽस्मि साङ्गोपाङ्गं वेदमधीये, मानवीयं धर्मशास्त्रं, माहेश्वरं योगशास्त्रं, बार्हस्पत्यमर्थशास्त्रं, मेधातिथेर्न्यायशास्त्रं प्राचेतसं श्राद्धकल्पं च" This *Medhatithi* ought to be an eminent *Maharshi* and not the commentator of *Manu*, for he is mentioned along with such high names as *Manu*, *Maheswara*, *Brihaspati* and *Prachetas*. Thus there is no reason for suspecting the age of *Bhasa* to be posterior to that of *Medhatithi*, the commentator of *Manu*.

7. The Merits of the works.

The characteristic merits of these *Natakas* are also in consonance with their extreme antiquity. The manner of expression in them is quite unique; for their language is so clear, lofty and majestic, as well as sweet and charming; and it is very seldom, if at all, that we meet with such excellences in works which are less than ten centuries old.

1. The sentences are everywhere replete with a wealth of ideas, beautifully expressed, which cultured minds will highly appreciate.

2, The varied and subtle manifestations of objects in different conditions and environments are graphically described, so as to be realized vividly by learned men.

3. Again, our celebrated poet who is always mindful of the *Rasas*, nowhere appears to be wanting in brevity or appropriateness of expression, nor does he fail to use adequate words or to convey proper meaning so as to suit the sentiments expressed.

4. It cannot be said that we do not meet with in the works of one or two very famous poets sweetness of expression or ease of language; but those qualities seem to have attained perfection in these dramatic works. That these dramas issued forth from the mouth of the poet as freely as breath itself,

will be apparent to all learned men on examination. In every way it appears to me that the elegance of diction as well as exposition in these dramas is only a different but a more pleasing form of Risbisuktis. On a close study of every one of these *Rupakas*, various merits herein detailed and even more can be easily discerned by all learned men. But I shall only quote a few *Vakyas* from everyone of these *Natakas* just to illustrate the flow of language.

The following verse taken from *Svapnavasavadatta* is addressed by *Yaugandharayana* to *Vasavadatta* who was sorely afflicted at b ing asked to get out of the way, in the forest by *Padmavati's* attendants—

"पूर्वं त्वयाप्यभिमतं गतमेवमासीच्छ्लाघ्यं गमिष्यसि पुनर्विजयेन भर्तुः ।
कालक्रमेण जगतः परिवर्तमाना चक्रारपङ्क्तिरिव गच्छति भाग्यपङ्क्तिः ॥"

The saying of *Vatsaraja* (Act 4, sl. 9) illustrates that a kind reception should meet with equal hospitality:—

"गुणानां वा विशालानां सत्काराणां च नित्यशः ।
कर्तारः सुलभा लोके विज्ञातारस्तु दुर्लभाः ॥"

The necessary results of labour are thus exemplified in *Pratijnanatika* (Act 1, sl. 18)—

"काष्ठादग्निर्जायते मथ्यमानाद् भूमिस्तोयं खन्यमाना ददाति ।
सोत्साहानां नास्त्यसाध्यं नराणां मार्गारब्धाः सर्वयत्नाः फलन्ति ।"

The following are the essentials of a bridegroom according to *Mahasena* (Act 2, sl. 4)—

"कुलं तावच्छ्लाघ्यं प्रथममभिकाङ्क्षे हि मनसा
ततः सानुक्रोशं मृदुरपि गुणो ह्येष बलवान् ।
ततो रूपे कान्तिं न खलु गुणतः स्त्रीजनभयात्
ततो वीर्योदग्रं न हि न परिपाल्या युवतयः ॥"

The feelings of a bride's mother are portrayed in (Act 2, sl 7)—

"अदत्तेत्यागता लज्जा दत्तेति व्यथितं मनः ।
धर्मस्नेहान्तरे न्यस्ता दुःखिताः खलु मातरः ॥"

The anxieties of a preceptor in reference to a pupil are described by *Dronacharya* in *Pancharatra* (Act 1, sl. 18)—

"अतीत्य बन्धूनवलङ्घ्य मित्राण्याचार्यमागच्छति शिष्यदोषः ।
बालं ह्यपत्यं गुरवे प्रदातुर्नैवापराधोऽस्ति पितुर्न मातुः ॥"

The next sloka (Act 2, sl, 9) brings out the fear of *Yudhishthira* lest the vices of *Dhartarashtras* should be imputed to them:—

"एकोदकत्वं खलु नाम लोके मनस्विनां कम्पयते मनांसि ।
वैरप्रियैस्तैर्हि कृतेऽपराधे यत्सत्यमस्माभिरिवापराद्धम् ॥"

Virata's praise of a warrior's deeds is contained in the following sloka (Act 2, sl, 28) —

"ताडितस्य हि योधस्य श्लाघनीयेन कर्मणा ।
अकालान्तरिता पूजा नाशयत्येव वेदनाम् ॥"

Here is a description of darkness as given in *Charudatta* (Act 1. sl. 20) —

"सुलभशरणमाश्रयो भयानां वनगहनं तिमिरं च तुल्यमेव ।
उभयमपि हि रक्षतेऽन्धकारो जनयति यश्च भयानि यश्च भीतः ॥"

The thougts of a thief are described in (Act 3. sl. 7.)—

"लुब्धोऽर्थवान् साधुजनाभिमानी वणिक् स्ववृत्तावतिकर्कशश्च ।
यस्तस्य गेहं यदि नाम लप्स्ये भवामि दुःखोपहतो न चित्ते ॥"

The following are *Dhritarashtra's* words of sorrow at *Abhimanu's* death, taken from *Dutaghatotkacha* (Sl. 17)—

"बहूनां समवेतानामेकस्मिन् निर्घृणात्मनाम् ।
बाले पुत्रे प्रहरतां कथं न पतिता भुजाः ॥"

Gahtaotkacha's retort to *Duryodhana* is given below(Sl. 45)—

न तु जतुगृहे सुप्तान् भ्रातॄन् निहन्ति निशाचराः
शिरसि न तथा भ्रातुः पत्नीं स्पृशन्ति निशाचराः ।
न च सुतवधं सङ्ख्ये वृत्तं स्मरन्ति निशाचराः
विकृतवपुषोऽप्युग्राचारा घृणा न तु वर्जिता ॥"

The heavy responsibilities of a king and a minister as described by them respectively are found in the following, from the *Avimaraka* (Act 1, Sls. 2 & 5)—

"धर्मः प्रागेव चिन्त्यः सचिवमतिगतिः प्रेक्षितव्या स्वबुद्ध्या
प्रच्छाद्यौ रागरोषौ मृदुपरुषगुणौ कालयोगेन कार्यौ ।
ज्ञेयं लोकानुवृत्तं परचरनयनैर्मण्डलं प्रेक्षितव्यं
रक्ष्यो यत्नादिहात्मा रणशिरसि पुनः सोऽपि नावेक्षितव्यः ॥
प्रसिद्धौ कार्याणां प्रवदति जनः पार्थिवबलं
विपत्तौ विस्पष्टं सचिवमतिदोषं जनयति ।
अमात्या इत्युक्ताः श्रुतिसुखमुदारं नृपतिभिः
सुसूक्ष्मं दण्ड्यन्ते गतिबलविदग्धाः कुपुरुषाः ॥"

The commencement of the night is described in (Act 2, Sl. 13)—

"व्यामृष्टसूर्यतिलको विततोडुमालो नष्टातपो मृदुमनोहरशीतवातः ।
संलीनकामुकजनः प्रविकीर्णचोरो वेषान्तरं रचयतीव मनुष्यलोकः ॥"

The supreme efficacy of fate is shown in the following verse (Act 3, sl. 12)—

"यत्ने कृते यदि न सिध्यति कोऽत्र दोषः
को वा न सिध्यति ममेति करोति यत्नम् ।
यत्नैः शुभैः पुरुषता भवतीह नृणां
दैवं विधानमनुगच्छति कार्यसिद्धिः ॥"

Efects of darkness are here depicted (*Balacharita*, Act 1, sl. 1[illegible] & Act 3, sl. 19)—

"अप्रकाशा इव दिशो घनीभूता इव द्रुमाः ।
सुनिविष्टस्य लोकस्य कृतो रूपविपर्ययः ॥"

"दुद्दिणविणठ्ठजोह्णा ळत्ती वट्टइ णिमीळिदाकाळा ।
संपाउदप्पसुत्ता णीळणिवषणा जहा गोवी ॥"

The benedictory verse in the *Madhyamavyayoga* runs as follows (Sl. 1)—

"पायात् सवोऽसुरवधूहृदयावसादः पादो हरेः कुवलयामलखड्गनीलः ।
यः प्रोद्यतस्त्रिभुवनैकमणे रराज वैदूर्यसंक्रम इवाम्बरसागरस्य ।।"

Here we have the description of a *Rakshasa* (sl. 26)—

"सिंहास्यः सिंहदंष्ट्रो मधुनिभनयनः स्निग्धगम्भीरकण्ठो
बभ्रुभ्रूः श्येननासो द्विरदपतिहनुर्दीर्घविश्लिष्टकेशः ।
व्यूढोरा वज्रमध्यो गजवृषभगतिर्लम्बपीनांसबाहुः
सुव्यक्तं राक्षसीजो विपुलबलयुतो लोकवीरस्य पुत्रः ।।"

Here is *Karna's* reply to *Salya* who objects to the giving away of his armour and ear-ring (*Karnabhara* Sl, 19)—

'शिक्षा क्षयं गच्छति कालपर्ययात् सुबद्धमूला निपतन्ति पादपाः ।
जलं जलस्थाना गतं च शुष्यति हुतं च दत्तं च तथैव तिष्ठति ।।"

The description of *Duryodhana* who has fallen down with his thigh broken is contained in this verse (*Urubhanga*, sl. 28)-

"श्रीमान् संयुगचन्दनेन रुधिरेणार्द्रानुलिप्तच्छवि-
भूसंसर्पणरेणुपाटलभुजो बालव्रतं ग्राहितः ।
निर्वृत्तेऽमृतमन्थने क्षितिधरान्मुक्तः सुरैः सासुरै-
राकर्षन्निव भोगमर्णवजले श्रान्तोज्झितो वासुकिः ।।"

The sorrowful words of *Lakshmana* as *Sita* faces the ordeal by fire (अग्निप्रवेश) are quoted below (*Abhishekanataka* Act 6, sl. 21)—

"विज्ञाय देव्याः शौचं च श्रुत्वाचार्यस्य शासनम् ।
धर्मस्नेहान्तरे न्यस्ता बुद्धिर्दोलायते मम ।।"

Ravana's words expressing that he need not anticipate any dangerous consequences from *Rama* are contained in Act 3, sl. 19.—

"कथं लम्बसटः सिंहो मृगेण विनिपात्यते ।
गजो वा सुमहान् मत्तः सृगालेन निहन्यते ।।"

Rama's utterance in *Pratimanataka* may be noted (Act 1, sl 4)—

"आरब्धे पटहे स्थिते गुरुजने भद्रासने लङ्घिते
स्कन्धाद्वारणनम्यमानवदनप्रच्योतितोये घटे ।
राज्ञाहूय विसर्जिते मयि जनो धैर्येण मे विस्मितः
स्वः पुत्रः कुरुते पितुर्यदि वचः कस्तत्र भो विस्मयः ॥"

The prostration of *Rama* at his father's feet immediately after he came to know of the royal mandate for his cororation as narrated to *Sita*, is described in these words (Act 1, sl. ι)—

"समं बाष्पेण पतता तस्योपरि ममाप्यधः ।
पितुर्मे क्लेदितौ पादौ ममापि क्लेदितं शिरः ॥"

The words addressed to *Rama* by *Lakshmana* who got extremely angry at *Kaikeyi's* conduct are as follows (Act 1, sl. 18)—

"यदि न सहसे राज्ञो मोहं धनुः स्पृश मा दया
स्वजननिभृतः सर्वोऽप्येवं मृदुः परिभूयते ।
अथ न रुचितं मुञ्च त्वं मामहं कृतनिश्चयो
युवतिरहितं कर्तुं लोकं यतश्छलिता वयम् ॥"

Bharata's feeling of surprise at the prospective sight of his own people may be quoted (Act ο, sl. 3) —

"पतितमिव शिरः पितुः पादयोः स्निह्यतेवास्मि राज्ञा समुत्थापित-
स्त्वरितमुपगता इव भ्रातरः क्लेदयन्तीव मामश्रुभिर्मातरः ।
सदृश इति महानिति व्यायतश्चेति भृत्यैरिवाहं स्तुतः सेवया
परिहसितमिवात्मनस्तत्र पश्यामि वेषं च भाषां च सौमित्रिणा ॥"

Bharata's reply to *Kaikeyi* may also be cited (Act, 3, sl, 16) —

"वयमयशसा चीरेणार्यो नृपो गृहमृत्युना
प्रततरुदितैः कृत्स्नायोध्या मृगैः सह लक्ष्मणः ।
दयिततनयाः शोकेनाम्बाः स्नुषाध्वपरिश्रमै-
र्धिगिति वचसा चोग्रेणात्मा त्वया ननु योजिताः ॥"

Here is another saying of *Bharata* (Act 3, sl. 22) —

"तत्र यास्यामि यत्रासौ वर्तते लक्ष्मणप्रियः ।
नायोध्या तं विनायोध्या सायोध्या यत्र राघवः ॥"

The benedictory verse in *Dutavakya* runs as follows:—

"पादः पायादुपेन्द्रस्य सर्वलोकोत्सवः स वः ।
व्याविद्धो नमुचिर्येन तनुताम्रनखेन खे ॥"

So far with reference to verses. The superior excellence of sentences which are not subject to the restrictions of versification is everywhere to be observed in these *Rupakas*. It really surpasses in grandeur the style of other works and is incomparable. A perusal of the work will make this clear; hence no illustrations are given.

8. Bhamaha's Criticism Explained.

The defects pointed out by *Bhamaha* in *Pratijna Natika* to which we have already referred, may be explained. Bhamaha considers it extremely improbable that such an illustrious king as *Vatsaraja* would have been unaware of his enemy's strategem in resorting to the fictitious elephant, either through the absence of spies or the negligence of his ministers; or that he would not have been murdered by his infuriated enemies, while he was alone and had fallen into their hands or that he could not have distinguished a ficititious elephant by day. The first statement does not require any serious refutation, for it is quite possible that even a farsighted king, with all his spies and his devoted and efficient ministers, in his great eagerness for elephant-hunt, might disregard his ministers' advice and proceed alone in haste.

Again, a prudent and generous-minded minister like *Salankayana* could well have prevented the attempted murder of *Vatsaraja* on the ground that it would be more pleasing to his lord if such a valiant and honourable foe could be taken captive, and that it would be a very mean act to kill a captive who was already stupefied by blows. It must be, for these reasons, that *Bhamahacharya* refers to the fictitious elephant as the last ground of his objections; but on a minute examination, even this is of no account, for in *Pratijna Natika*, *Hamsaka*, in reference to deception practised upon *Vatsaraja*, speaks:—

"तदो दिउणं बि अ अद्धाणं गच्छिअ साळलुक्खच्छाआए सवण्णणहणीळदाए परुब्भासिदेहि असरीरविणिक्खित्तेहि विअ दन्तजुअळेहि सूइदो षणुस्सदमत्तेण विअ दिट्ठो सो दिव्ववारणपडिच्छन्दो ।"

It is clear from the above passage that the place where the fictitious black elephant was posted, was covered with such a dense forest of sala trees that it was hardly possible to distinguish an elephant. While even the existence of the elephant was left to be inferred only through the tusks, it were hardly likely to conceive even by day that it might possibly be a fictitious one. It is, however, clear from *Pratijna Natika* that *Vatsaraja's* elephant-hunt must have taken place about mid-day. From this, *Bhamaha* concludes that, however dense the trees might be, even there, darkness cannot co-exist with mid-day light, that it is thus impossible that an elephant could not be distinguished owing to the density of the sala trees, and that such a statement is a mere exaggeration. On the other hand, it seems to us that actual experience shows that there could be total darkness on account of the density of sala trees, in spite of broad day light. If on the other hand, as narrated in the *Kathasaritsagara* which is a close copy of *Brihatkatha*, evening twilight had begun to set in, *Vatsaraja's* erroneous impression becomes more probable; but this ingenious statement does nowhere appear in *Pratijna Natika*, and that it is quite possible that the author of the *Brihatkatha* might have conceived this statement for the sake of repelling *Bhamaha's* criticisms and *Somedevabhatta* having come across it in *Brihatkatha* would have inserted it in his own work, *Kathasaritsagara*. * Everything has thus been rendered clear.

---

* II. Lambaka, IV. Taranaga, XVIII, Sloka

"गान्धर्वदत्तचित्तत्वात् सन्ध्याध्वान्तवशाच्च सः ।

न तं वनगतं राजा मायागजमलक्षयत् ॥"

There is no path trodden by great poets like *Kalidasa*, but is pioneered by *Bhasa*. There are many points of similarity to *Bhasa's* work in *Abhijnanasakuntala* the best known works of *Kalidasa* who has attained unrivalled fame as the prince of poets, since the era of *Vikramaditya*.

9. Bhasa's followers.

For example, a sloka in the fourth act of *Abhishekanataka* runs thus :—

"यस्यां न प्रियमण्डनापि महिषी देवस्य मन्दोदरी
स्नेहाल्लुम्पति पल्लवान् न च पुनर्वीजन्ति यस्यां भयात् ।
वीजन्तो मलयानिला अपि करैरस्पृष्टबालद्रुमा
सेयं शक्ररिपोरशोकवनिका भग्नेति विज्ञाप्यताम् ॥"

There is a similar verse in the fourth act of *Sakuntala* :—

"पातुं न प्रथमं व्यवस्यति पयो युष्मास्वपीतेषु या
नादत्ते प्रियमण्डनापि भवतां स्नेहेन या पल्लवम् ।
आद्ये वः कुसुमप्रसूतिसमये यस्या भवत्युत्सवः
सेयं याति शकुन्तला पतिगृहं सर्वैरनुज्ञायताम् ॥"

Here it may be observed that there is not only similarity of ideas between the two slokas but the very same sweet and melodious expressions, such as प्रियमण्डनापि स्नेहात्, पल्लवान्, सेयं, are used by *Kalidasa* also. Again in the first act of *Balacharita*, the following verse has reference to *Devaki*, who, having entrusted the child to *Vasudeva* seems, as it were, to proceed towards two different directions; her body going towards the place of confinement, but her mind towards the child :—

"हृदयेनेह तत्राङ्गैर्द्विधाभूतेव गच्छति ।
यथा नभसि तोये च चन्द्रलेखा द्विधा कृता ॥"

There is a striking similarity between this verse and the following one in the first act of *Sakuntala* :—

"गच्छति पुरः शरीरं धावति पश्चादसंस्तुतं चेतः ।
चीनांशुकमिव केतोः प्रतिवातं नीयमानस्य ॥

The following line in the first act of *Svapnavasavadatta*,

"विस्रब्धं हरिणाश्चरन्त्यचकिता देशागतप्रत्ययाः ।'

is by a slight change rendered thus in the first act of *Sakuntala* :—

"विश्वासोपगमादभिन्नगतयः शब्दं सहन्ते मृगाः"

Similarly there may be observed several other points of resemblance between the works of *Bhasa* and those of *Kalidasa*.

Again such striking similarities can be clearly noticed in *Bhavabhuti's* works also on a close examination. As instances may be taken *Atreyi's* discourse in the second act of *Uttararamacharita* which closely follows that of the *Brahmacharin* in the first act of *Svapnavasavadatta*, as also that of the *Vidyadhara* in the sixth act which follows a similar discourse in the sixth act of *Abhishekanataka*.

Again, the use of *Dandaka* in the fifth act of *Malatimadhava* bears a strong analogy to the *Dandaka* form employed in the fifth act of *Avimaraka*.

The work known as *Mrichchhakatika* which is reputed to be older than *Kalidasa's* plays not only contains many points

10. Mrichchhakatika Compared

of similarity to *Bhasa's* works but the very same sentences are taken wholesale from the one in the other. Thus several verses and sentences in *Charudattanataka* are either literally transcribed, or are made to undergo but slight alteration in *Mrichchhakatika*.

A verse in the first act of *Charudattanataka* runs thus :—

"यासां बलिर्भवति मद्गृहदेहलीनां हंसैश्च सारसगणैश्च विभक्तपुष्पः ।

तास्वेव पूर्वबलिरूढयवाङ्कुरासु बीजाञ्जलिः पतति कीटमुखावलीढः ॥"

The corresponding verse in *Mrichchhakatika* is the following :—

"यासां बलिः सपदि मद्गृहदेहलीनां हंसैश्च सारसगणैश्च विलुप्तपूर्वः ।
तास्वेव सम्प्रति विरूढतृणाङ्कुरासु बीजाञ्जलिः पतति कीटमुखावलीढः ॥

Again in the third act of *Charudattanataka*, the following sloka occurs :—

"मार्जारः प्लवने वृकोऽपसरणे श्येनो गृहालोकने
निद्रा सुप्तमनुष्यवीर्यतुलने संसर्पणे पन्नगः ।
माया वर्णशरीरभेदकरणे वाग् देशभाषान्तरे
दीपो रात्रिषु संकटे च तिमिरं वायुः स्थले नौर्जले ॥

The third act of *Mrichchhakatika* also contains a sloka corresponding to it :—

"मार्जारः क्रमणे मृगः प्रसरणे श्येनो गृहालुञ्चने
सुप्तासुप्तमनुष्यवीर्यतुलने श्वा सर्पणे पन्नगः ।
माया रूपशरीरवेषरचने वाग् देशभाषान्तरे
दीपो रात्रिषु संकटेषु डुडुभो वाजी स्थले नौर्जले ॥

Similarly in the fourth act of *Charudatta* and *Mrichchhakatika* respectively there are the following slokas :—

"विषादस्रस्तसर्वाङ्गी सम्भ्रमोत्फुल्ललोचना
मृगीव शरविद्धाङ्गी कम्पसे चानुकम्पसे ॥ "
"विषादस्रस्तसर्वाङ्गी सम्भ्रमभ्रान्तलोचना ।
नीयमाना भुजिष्या त्वं कम्पसे नानुकम्पसे ॥"

These are the words of *Sutradhara* in *Charudatta* :—

"किण्णुखु अज्ज पच्चूस एव्व गेहादो निक्खन्तस्स बुभुक्खाए पुक्खरपत्तपडिद-जळविन्दू विअ चळचळाअन्ति विअ मे अक्खीणि। (परिक्रम्य) जाव गेहं गच्छिअ

जाणामि किण्णुखु संविधा विहिदा णवेत्ति। एदं अह्माणं गेहं। जाव पविसामि ॥"

The same idea is expressed in *Mrichchhakatika* in the following terms :—

"......चिरसङ्गीदोवासणेण सुक्खपोक्खरणालाइं विअ मे बुभुक्खाए मिळाणाइं अच्छादं। ता जाव गेहं गदुअ आणामि अत्थि किं पि कुटुम्बिणीए उववादिअं ण वेत्ति। (परिक्रम्यावलोक्य च) एदं तं अह्माणं गेहं। ता पविसामि।"

At the beginning of the second act of *Charudatta* occur the following sentences :—

"गणिका — तदो तदो।

चेटी — अह्महे! ण किञ्चि मए भणिदं। किं तदो तदोत्ति।

गणिका — हञ्जे! किं मए मन्तिदं।"

Similar expressions occur in *Mrichchhakatika* also,

"वसन्तसेना — हञ्जे! तदो तदो।

चेटी — अज्जुए! ण किं पि मन्तेसि। किं तदो तदो।

वसन्तसेना — किं मए भणिदं।

चेटी — तदो तदो तदो त्ति।"

Again, the third act of *Charudatta* contains the folloiwng,

"चारुदत्तः — वयस्य! वीणा नामासमुद्रोत्थितं रत्नम्। कुतः"

"विदूषकः — कामं पसंसेदु भवं। मम खु दाव माअन्तो मणुस्सो इत्थिआ वि पठन्ती उभअं आदरं ण देदि। गाअन्तो दाव मणुस्सो रत्तसुमणावेढ्ढिदो विअ पुरोहिदो दिढं णसोभइ। इत्थिआ वि पठन्ती छिण्णणासा विअ धेणुआ अदिविरूव होइ ॥"

Similarly in *Mrishchhakatika* :—

चारुदत्तः — अहो अहो साधु साधु रेभिलेन गीतम्। वीणा हि नामासमुद्रोत्थितं रत्नम्। कुतः"

"विदूषकः — मम दाव दुवेहिं जेव्व हस्सं जाअदि। इत्थिआए सक्कअं पठन्तीए मणुस्सेण अ काअलिं गाअन्तेण। इत्थिआ दाव सक्कअं पठन्ती दिण्णणवणस्सा विअ गिट्ठी अहिअं सुसुहाअदि। मणुस्सा वि काअलिं गाअन्तो सुक्खसुमणोदामवेढ्ढिदो वुड्ढपुरोहिदो विअ मन्तं जवन्तो दिढं मे ण रोअदि।"

The fourth act of *Charudatta* has the following :—

"सज्जलकः — मदनिके ! किं न पर्याप्तं, द्वितीयमप्यनार्यं करिष्यामि । न खल्वत्र शस्त्रेण कश्चित् परिक्षतो व्यापादितो वा ।"

Similar words in *Mrichchhakatika* are :—

"शर्विलकः — मदनिके ! भीते सुप्ते न शर्विलकः प्रहरति । तन्मया न कश्चिद् व्यापादितो नापि परिक्षतः ।"

Another sentence in the fourth act of *Charudatta* runs as follows :—

"सज्जलकः — आर्यचारुदत्तेनास्मि प्रेषितः, यस्तावदलङ्कारो मम हस्ते निक्षिप्तः, स स्वयं भोगमलिनतया गृहस्यासान्निध्यात् कौटुम्बिकानां दुरारक्षः । तद् गृह्यतामिति ।"

The analogous passage in *Mrichchhakatika* runs thus :—

"शर्विलकः — सार्थवाहस्त्वां विज्ञापयति — जर्जरत्वाद् गृहस्य दूरक्षमिदं भाण्डम् । तद् गृह्यतामिति ॥"

Many other analogous passages can be easily pointed out. Again, the plot in both the plays centres round *Charudatta*. It thus follows that one should be the basis of the other. It may, however, be appropriate to observe that *Charudatta nataka* alone can be the source wherefrom *Mrichchhakatika* is derived; for it is only in later-day plays that the work and its author are specially mentioned. While the *Prastavana* in *Mrichchhakatika* contains a description of the poet and his work, the same is wanting in *Charudatta* which only goes to show that the former is of subsequent date. However, *Mrichchhakatika* contains many excellent passages which are not met with in *Charudatta*. Hence the proper inference seems to be that the short play of *Charudatta* has been amply enlarged by the addition of fine passages which renders the plot even more interesting and has, under the name of *Mrichchhakatika*, become famous as the work of *Sudraka*. Thus *Mrichchhakatika* being almost another version of *Charudatta*, it is but proper that learned men should regard it as a very ancient work and its author as belonging to a very remote period under the false impression that he is the original author, though his work simply consisted in rebuilding with old materials. There is no authority to say that *Sudraka* must have lived prior to *Kalidasa*, but it is certain that he is a predecessor of *Vamana*, the Rhetorician; for he expressly says in his *Kavyalankarasutravritti*:—

"शूद्रकादिरचितेषु प्रबन्धेष्वस्य (श्लेषाख्यगुणस्य) भूयान् प्रपञ्चो दृश्यते ।"
Thus it is clear that the poetical eminence of *Bhasa* has been the mainstay of poets like *Kalidasa* and *Sudraka*.

11. The merits of Pratima and Svapna; Kalidasa's Dependence on Bhasa.

Looking into the composition of *Bhasa* it will be seen that his unrivalled merit lies in the delineation of the real nature of things in their conditions by sweet, apt and lucid words suggestive of lofty ideas. Of the natakas of *Bhasa* hitherto obtained, wherein this merit of his shines most, one is the *Svapnavasavadatta* and the other, I think, is the *Pratimanataka*. Of these two, in the *Svapnavasavadatta*, the central *Rasa* (रस) is the *Vipralambhasringara* (विप्रलम्भश्रृङ्गार) to which the *Arthasringara* (अर्थश्रृङ्गार) is only an auxiliary. In the *Pratima*, however, the central Rasa that runs through it is the *Dharmavira* mingled with *Karuna Rasa*—the *Dharmavira* manifesting itself in the enthusiasm displayed by the hero in cherishing the single thought of carrying out the *Dharma*, i. e., fulfilling the mandates of his royal father. The life-like reality of soliloquy and conversation in these *Natakas* is quite unparalleled, and so is their attraction for men of discernment. Some of the materials of these *Natakas* which completely engross the minds of the readers are found to have been shadowed forth in the *Sakuntala*. In the *Pratimanataka*:—

(1) The incident of the *Valkala* described in the first Act is also seen in the first act of *Sakuntala*. The thought concisely expressed by *Bhasa* in "सव्वसोहणीअं सुरूवं णाम" (*Pratima*, Act. I) is taken up by *Kalidasa* and conveyed in the form, (Act 1, sl. 17)

" किमिव हि मधुराणां मण्डनं नाकृतीनाम् ।"

and is enlarged on by such illustrations as that of lotus etc., thus,

"सरसिजमनुविद्धं शैवलेनापि रम्यं
मलिनमपि हिमांशोर्लक्ष्म लक्ष्मीं तनोति ।
इयमधिकमनोज्ञा वल्कलेनापि तन्वी"

(ii) The penance of watering plants described in the fifth act is found in the first act of the *Sakuntala* with just this difference, that, whereas *Bhasa* has described the penance as being bearable, in apt *Arthantaranyasa* containing *Upama* (*Pratima*, Act 5, sl 9),

"योऽस्याः करः श्राम्यति दर्पणेऽपि स नैति खेदं कलशं वहन्त्याः ।
कष्टं वनं स्त्रीजनसौकुमार्यं समं लताभिः कठिनीकरोति ॥"

the unbearableness of the same is expressed by *Kalidasa* in the form of a *Nidarsana* (*Sakuntala*, Act 1, sl. 16)

"इदं किलाव्याजमनोहरं वपुस्तपःक्षमं साधयितुं य इच्छति ।
ध्रुवं स नीलोत्पलपत्रधारया समिल्लतां छेत्तुमृषिर्व्यवस्यति ॥"

The heroes also in both the works equally applaud the penance, with the friendly greetings "अपि तपोवर्धते" (*Pratima* Act V and *Sakuntala* Act I). Besides in the couplet occurring in the same act of *Pratimanataka*, (Act 5, sl. 11)

"आपृच्छ पुत्रकृतकान् हरिणान् द्रुमांश्च
विन्ध्यं वनं तव सखीर्दयिता लताश्च ॥"

Rama asks *Sita* to bid good-bye to the fawns and trees, which she had tended as her foster-children, to the Vindhya mountain and the creepers, her dearest friends. Among these, the taking leave of the trees as foster-children is plainly described in the *Sakuntala* (Act 4, sl. 8)

"भो भोः सन्निहितदेवतास्तपोवनतरवः !
पातुं न प्रथमं व्यवस्यति जलं युष्मास्वपीतेषु या
नादत्ते प्रियमण्डनापि भवतां स्नेहेन या पल्लवम् ।

आद्ये वः कुसुमप्रसूतिसमये यस्या भवत्युत्सवः
सेयं याति शकुन्तला पतिगृहं सर्वैरनुज्ञायताम् ॥ ''

while the idea of taking leave of the fawns and creepers is suggested by way of their remembrance during *Sakuntala's* departure, (Act, 4, sl. 13 & 11)

'' जहाति सोऽयं न पुत्रकृतकः पदवीं मृगस्ते ''

'' मुञ्चन्दि अस्सूणि विअ वणळदाओ ''

(iii) In the following sentence addressed by *Rama* to *Sita* in the seventh act of *Pratima Nataka*,

'' अभ्युपलभ्यतेऽस्य सप्तपर्णस्याधस्ताच्छुक्लवाससं भरतं दृष्ट्वा परित्रस्तं मृगयूथमासीत् । ''

Sita is reminded of the want of confidence towards *Bharata* diplayed by the deer herd; while in the fifth act of the *Sakuntala Dushshanta* is reminded of the same incident towards him displayed by the fawn, in an exquisitely different form in the following words of *Sakuntala*,

'' तक्खणं खु सो मम दीहापङ्गो णाम किदअपुत्तओ उवट्ठिदो । तुए अयं दाव पढमं पिवदु त्ति अणुअम्पिणा उवच्छन्दिदो उदएण, ण उण दे अपरिअआदो हत्थब्भासं उवगओ । पच्छा तस्सिं एव्व मए गहीदे सळिळे किदो देण पणओ । तदो इत्थं परिहसिदो सि । सव्वो सगन्धेसु विस्ससदि । दुवे वि एत्थ आरण्णआ त्ति । ''

In the above passage the confidence of the deer in the forest-dwellers is explicitly expressed in actual words, while in the *Pratimanataka* on the other hand, the same idea is suggesed by the sense.

In the *Svapnavasavadatta*:—

(i) The incident of meeting the ascetics in the hermitage described in the first act is also found in the first act of the *Sakuntala*. There the heroine, *Padmavati*, being thus addressed by the lady-ascetic, (*Svapna*, Act 1)

'' पविस जादे! पविस । तवोवणाणि णाम अदिहिजणस्स सअगेहं । ''

replies

'' भोदु भोदु अय्ये! विस्सत्थम्हि । इमिणा बहुमाणवअणेण अणुग्गहिदम्हि ''

The very same idea is conveyed, in a different manner in the following words of the king satisfied with the hospitality of *Anasuya*, (*Sakuntala*, Act 1)

" भवतु । भवतीनां सूनृतयैव गिरा कृतमातिथ्यम् । "

Again, consider the words of the chamberlain advising the servant to desist from causing obstruction to the dwellers of the hermitage, (*Svapna* Act 1, sl. 5)

" नखलु नखलूत्सारणा कार्या । पश्य,

परिहरतु भवान् नृपापवादं न परुषमाश्रमवासिषु प्रयोज्यम् ।
नगरपरिभवान् विमोक्तुमेते वनमभिगम्य मनस्विनो वसन्ति ॥ "

The very same idea is shadowed forth in the following words addressed by the king to his commander-in-chief, in the *Sakuntala*, (Act 2, sl. 7)

" यथाच सैनिकास्तपोवनं दूरादेव परिहरन्ति, तथा निषेद्धव्याः । पश्य,

" शमप्रधानेषु तपोधनेषु गूढं हि दाहात्मकमस्ति तेजः ।
स्पर्शानुकूला इव सूर्यकान्तास्तदन्यतेजोभिभवाद वमन्ति ॥ "

In the former passage the advice to desist from offending the residents of the hermitage is given in view of the respect due to their serenity; while in the latter the same is impelled by the fear of the strength of their penance. This idea too is doubtless implied in the epithet मनस्विन् occurring in the former.

(ii) The merrymaking words of the female friend towards *Padmavati*, during her pastime with the ball, occurring in the second act of the *Svapnavasavadatta*,

" पद्मावदी — अय्ये ! किं दाणिं मं ओहसिदुं विअ णिज्झाअसि ।

वासवदत्ता — णहि णहि । हळा ! अधिअं अज्ज सोहदि । अभिदो विअ दे अज्ज वरमुहं पेक्खामि ।

पद्मावती — अवेहि । मा दाणिं मं ओहस । "

have reference to the attainment of a bridegroom, while in the *Sakuntala* the same idea occurs in the scene of watering the shrubs by the heroine, (Act 1)

"प्रियंवदा — (सस्मितम्) अणसूए! जाणासि किं सउन्दळा वणजोसिणिं अदिमेत्तं पेक्खदित्ति।

अनसूया — णहु विभावेमि। कहेहि।

प्रियंवदा — जइ वणजोसिणी अत्तणो सदिसेण पाअवेण सङ्गदा, अविणाम एव्वं अहं वि अत्तणो अणुरूवं वरं लभेअत्ति।

शकुन्तला — एसो णूणं तुइ अत्तगदो मणारहो।"

(iii) The imaginary herbs *Avidhavakarana* and *Sapatnimardana* referred to in the third act have for their counterpart the amulet *Aparajita*, in the seventh act of *Sakuntala*.

(iv) In the sixth act, the love of *Vatsaraja* towards *Vasavadatta* is heightened by the incident of the regaining of the *Vina* (वीणा) which was lost at first, and by obtaining subsequently the picture of *Vasavadatta*; while in the sixth act of the *Sakuntala*, the recovery of the lost ring and the subsequent gain of *Sakuntala's* picture, both similar in nature to the above said incidents, are introduced to intensify the love of *Dushshanta*. Further the feelings of condolence and censure portrayed in respect of the *Vina* in the *Svapnanataka* is similarly displayed in regard to the ring in the *Sakuntala*.

Condolence is thus described in the *Svapnanataka*,

(Act 6, sl 1)

"श्रुतिसुखनिनदे! कथं नु देव्याः स्तनयुगले जघनस्थले च सुप्ता।
विहगगणरजोविकीर्णदण्डा प्रतिभयमध्युषितास्यरण्यवासम्॥"

Its parallel runs thus in the *Sakuntala* (Act. 6, sl. 11)

"तव सुचरितमङ्गुलीय! नूनं प्रतनु ममेव विभाव्यते फलेन।
अरुणनखमनोहरासु तस्याश्च्युतमसि लब्धपदं यदङ्गुलीषु॥"

Here the unhappy lot of the ring is explicitly described in actual words, and beautified by an *Upama*; while that of the *Vina* in the *Svapnanataka* is with great effect suggested. Censure is thus conveyed in the *Svapnanataka*. (Act 6, Sl 2)

"राजा — अस्निग्धासि घोषवति! या तपस्विन्या न स्मरसि।

"श्रोणीसमुद्वहनपार्श्वनिपीडितानि स्वेदस्तनान्तरसुखान्युपगूहितानि।
उद्दिश्य मां च विरहे परिदेवितानि वाद्यान्तरेषु कथितान्यपि सस्मितानि॥"

The same feeling is thus depicted in the *Svapnanataka* (Act 6, sl. 13)

"कथं नु तं बन्धुरकोमलाङ्गुलिं करं विहायासि निमग्नमम्भसि ।

अथवा,

"अचेतनं नाम गुणं न लक्षयेन्मयैव कस्मादवधीरिता प्रिया ॥"

Here in the above verse the speaker is beside himself with love in the first half but wakes up in the second half while the difference in the portrayal of the censure expressed in respect of *Ghoshavati* is that the unconsciousness is kept up to the end.

Although the incident of the curse of *Durvasa* and the happy reunion of the lovers at the door of *Maricha*, found in the *Sakuntala*, follow the *Avimaraka* where the curse of *Chandabhargava* and the meeting again of the lovers at the door of *Narada* are described, and in the same manner traces of the imitation of ideas contained in the *Abhishekanataka* and *Balacharita* also exist in the *Sakuntala* (vide introduction to the *Svapnavasavadatta*); nevertheless from the fact that *Sakuntala* is mostly embellished only with the ideas contained in the *Svapna* and *Pratima Natakas*, it is certain that the mind of *Kalidasa* must have been strongly attracted by the poetic excellences of these two works. Again, their ideas have been adopted by *Kalidasa* not only in his dramatic composition, but also in his lyric and epic poems. For the sense contained in the following couplet occurring in the *Svapnanataka*, (Act 1, sl. 4)

"कालक्रमेण जगतः परिवर्तमाना चक्रारपङ्क्तिरिव गच्छति भाग्यपङ्क्तिः ।"

is extracted in the following words of the *Meghaduta* (*Uttaramegha*, sl. 46),

"कस्यात्यन्तं सुखमुपनतं दुःखमेकान्ततो वा
नीचैर्गच्छत्युपरि च गतिश्चक्रनेमिक्रमेण ।"

In the seventh act of *Pratimanataka*, *Rama* says to *Sita* knowing already that *Bharata* is coming to receive him (*Pratima*, Act 7, sl. 4),

"रेणुः समुत्पतति लोध्रसमानगौरः संप्रावृणोति च दिशः पवनावधूतः ॥"

The very same idea occurs, with slight difference, in the same context, in the *Raghuvamsa* (*Raghu*, 13, 64)

"विरक्तसन्ध्याकपिशं पुरस्ताद् यथा रजः पार्थिवमुज्जिहीते ।
शङ्के हनूमत्कथितप्रवृत्तिः प्रत्युद्गतो मां भरतः ससैन्यः ॥"

The narration of great-great-grandfather, great-grandfather, grandfather and father, *Dilipa*, *Raghu*, *Aja* and *Dasaratha* found in the *Pratimanataka* is mentioned in the order found in the *Raghuvamsa* and not in the order of the *Ramayana*. Thus many other instances of the influence of *Bhasa* are observeable in the poems of *Kalidasa*. Hence, it is clear that *Kalidasa* has the same high regard for *Bhasa*, as he has for *Valmiki* and *Vyasa*; for he depends, for his poetical excellence, as much upon *Bhasa*, as upon *Valmiki* and *Vyasa*.

The imitation of *Valmiki* is seen in the *Sakuntala* (Act 3, sl. 4)

"शक्यमरविन्दसुरभिः कणवाही मालिनीतरङ्गाणाम् ।
अङ्गैरनङ्गततैरविरलमालिङ्गितुं पवनः ॥"

Compare, side by side, with this, the original in the *Ramayana* (4, 28),

"मेघोदरविनिर्मुक्ताः कल्हारसुखशीतलाः ।
शक्यमञ्जलिभिः पातुं वाताः केतकिगन्धिनः ॥"

Here, the wind's being worthy of being best enjoyed is described in general forms in "अञ्जलिभिः पातुं शक्यम्" while the same is expressed in the previous verse in the particular form of the winds fit to be incessantly embraced. The extraction of the very words themselves is plain.

The imitation of the ideas of *Vyasa* is seen in the *Kumarasambhava*, when the *Saptarshis* praise *Siva* (6, 21)

"या नः प्रीतिर्विरूपाक्ष ! तव निध्यानसम्भवा ।
सा किमावेद्यते तुभ्यमन्तरात्मासि देहिनाम् ॥"

The original of the above verse is found in the *Mahabharata* where *Vidura* praises *Sri Krishna* (Udyoga 91, 30),

"या मे प्रीतिः पुष्कराक्ष! त्वद्दर्शनसमुद्भवा ।
सा किमाख्यायते तुभ्यमन्तरात्मासि देहिनाम् ॥"

That almost everything contained in the above is embodied in the previous verse is plain.

12. Dingnaga.

There is a tradition that a certain *Dingnagacharya*, a contemporary of *Kalidasa*, used to find fault with the writngs of *Kalidasa*, to which, while commenting on the line in the *Meghaduta*,

"दिङ्नागानां पथि पडिहरन् स्थूलहस्तावलेपान् ।"

Mallinatha refers thus,

'दिङ्नागाचार्यस्य कालिदासप्रतिपक्षस्य हस्तावलेपान् हस्तविन्यासपूर्वकाणि दूषणानि परिहरन्'

while *Dakshinavarta* * commenting on the above line of *Kalidasa* thus,

"दिङ्नाग इति कोऽप्याचार्यः कालिदासप्रबन्धान् अन्यत्रोक्तोऽयमर्थ इति स्थूलहस्ताभिनयैर्दूषयति ।"

refers to the adaptation of the thoughts of others as the reason for such fault-finding. This adaptation of the thoughts of others must only be the imitation of the ideas of *Bhasa* and others above pointed out. Nevertheless, though blamed by *Dingnaga* for this reason, yet on account of the fact that *Kalidasa* has combined in his poetical compositions, to an extraordinary degree, the sweetness of verse, an intensity of poetic merit characteristic of archaic poetical writings and the qualities which furnish supreme relief to men of critical faculty, his works were appreciated beyond measure by *Nichula* and other poets, and also by all lovers of Sanskrit. It was due to this that *Dingnaga's* fault-finding attitude towards *Kalidasa* has very little effect. In fact, *Valmiki*, *Vyasa* and *Bhasa* who are archaic poets deserve to be imitated on the ground that they were pioneers of ancient poetical thought. Thus we find, that *Asvaghosha*, a poet who is said to have

* Vide p. 13, Trivandrum Sanskrit Series No. 64.

flourished in the first century B. C., has transformed the verse of *Bhasa* (*Pratijna*, 1-18)

"काष्ठादग्निर्जायते मथ्यमानाद् भूमिस्तोयं खन्यमाना ददाति ।
सोत्साहानाम् नास्त्यसाध्यं नराणां मार्गारब्धाः सर्वयत्नाः फलन्ति ॥"

into the following verse in the 13th Sarga of his *Buddha-charita*,

"काष्ठं हि मथ्नन् लभते हुताशं भूमिं खनन् विन्दति चापि तोयम् ।
निर्बन्धिनः किञ्चन नास्त्यसाध्यं न्यायेन युक्तं च कृतं च सर्वम् ॥"

Of these, the first could never fail to strike the scholar as the original, from its easy graceful flow; and the other, as the borrowed one, being otherwise. Hence an imitation of their writings was only held in esteem by *Kalidasa*, *Nichula* and others. In truth, *Dingnaga's* attitude towards *Kalidasa* was due only to his fault-finding propensity.

The archaic elegance of the writings of the *Rishis*, found in the poetical compositions of *Bhasa* has been referred to by me as entitling him to be placed on a level with the *Rishis*, in my introduction to the *Svapnavasavadatta*. Now, we infer that there must have been a tradition of old describing him as a *Muni*. For *Jonaraja* (15th century A. D.) a commentator of the *Prithvirajacharita* written by *Jayanaka* in the 12th century A. D. styles *Bhasa* as a Muni while commenting on the following verse* (Prithvirajacharita, 1, 3),

13. Bhasa, A Rishi.

"सत्काव्यसंहारविधौ खलानां दीप्तानि वह्नेरपि मानसानि ।
भासस्य काव्यं खलु विष्णुधर्मान् (?) सोऽप्याननात् पारतवन्मुमोच ॥"

The commentary on the above verse runs thus:—

"सतां काव्यं, तद्विषये संहारविधौ दाहे दोषारोपणेऽग्नेरपि सकाशात् दुर्जनानां चित्तानि दीप्तान्यजडानि भवन्ति। अत्र साधनमाह — सोऽग्निरपि भासमुनेः काव्यं विष्णुधर्मान् मुखात् त्यक्तवान् नादहदित्यर्थः । पारतवदित्युपमा । अग्निर्हि वस्त्वन्तरवत् पारतं दग्धुमशक्तो मुखान्मुञ्चति । भासव्यासयाः काव्यविषये स्पर्धा

---

* Vide Appendix II, (b)

कुर्वतोः सर्वोत्कर्षवर्तित्वेन परीक्षकान्तराभावात् परीक्षार्थमग्निमध्ये तयोर्द्वयोः काव्यद्वयं क्षिप्तम् । तयोर्मध्यादग्निर्विष्णुधर्मान्नादहदिति प्रसिद्धिः । *खलैस्तु प्राप्तं सत्काव्यं दह्यत इत्यग्नेः सकाशात् खलानां दाहकत्वमित्यर्थः ॥ "

Although the epithet *Rishi* is applicable chiefly to seers of vedic hymns, yet on account of the fact that the term has largely come to be used in course of time to those to whom only the epithet *Muni* would be actually applicable, the epithets *Muni* and *Rishi* could very well be treated as being quite synonymous. In any way, having in view that people submit to any innovation in the field of the usage of words made by a *Muni* in the same way as in the case of a *Rishi*, without making a difference between the two, we have used the terms here as being identical in meaning.

In connection with *Bhasa* being regarded as a Rishi, it may be said that it is quite proper that usages which depart from the operation of the rules of *Panini* are largely found in *Bhasa*, as in the writings of other *Rishis*; and his works are highly approved of by such close followers of *Panini* as *Kalidasa*, *Bhattabana* and others with the same regard that they have for the writings of other *Rishis*. The dry word-reasoning reconciling certain of such usages to the precepts of *Panini*, referred to in the introduction to the *Svapnanataka*, is merely an imitation of the twisted and strained interpretation of the modern grammarians. Neither does such reasoning appeal to lovers of Sanskrit, nor, on the other hand, do such usages cease to be deprived of their peculiarity and become common usages. In fact, numerous ‡ archaisms are still found in *Bhasa's* compositions, which are beyond the range of such plausible justifications as the above and which cannot be explained away as the mistakes of the scribes. Hence, it is not incompatible that *Bhasa* with his status as a *Rishi*, should be a forerunner in the field of *Drisyakavya* inasmuch as *Valmiki* and *Vyasa* are in the field of *Sravyakavya*. For this reason, the appropriateness of the imitation of *Bhasa* by *Kalidasa* who followed him should be regarded as being

* Vide Appendix II (b)

‡ Vide Appendix I.

well established, in the same manner as the appropriateness of the imitation of the writings of *Valmiki* and *Vyasa* by *Bhasa* who came after them.

14. Comparison of Bhasa and Kalidasa

Further, *Rupakas*, as they exhibit before us events which occurred away from us, are styled as *Drisya* (visible) compositions. The impression thus created by the exhibition is the *Rasa* which highly captivates the mind. It is on this ground that a combination of only such materials, as conduce to the creation of the *Rasa*, deserves to be introduced into the *Rupakas*. This is effected by depicting without any effort before the minds of the observers, the materials taken up without divesting them of their natural colour. Therefore it is that such of them as could be depicted only in an artifical colour should be discarded by poets, and the highest natural beauty of the materials should be depicted. The exquisiteness of their innate qualities should not be veiled over by incoherent rhetorical arrangement. On the other hand, it might be embellished in some places, when desirable, by appropriate figures of speech introduced with graceful ease. This method has been cleverly adopted by *Bhasa*, while to some extent by *Kalidasa*. The utterances of *Bhasa* are mostly quite elegant but not rhetorically polished, while those of *Kalidasa* shine by rhetorical gloss. The figures of speech that have been used by *Bhasa* are only *Upama* (उपमा), *Arthantaranyasa* (अर्थान्तरन्यास) and others of the kind, which are employed in common parlance by all, and are easily understandable; and these too are drawn without effort, and only in small numbers here and there; while on the other hand they are introduced by *Kalidasa* with effort in many places. This will be readily perceived by a cursory glance of the *Kavyas* of the two writers and as such is not exemplified here.

Further, all the ideas pertaining to a dramatic composition should be impressed on the observers with a natural vividness by the elegance of the mental soliloquy and of the conversations of the *dramatis personae*. As the sense of the ideas conveyed should express the practice of the world at large, similarly the language in which the sense is couched should conform to the trend of daily occurrences. As the language adopted in conversations by the people is in the form of prose, it follows that prose is the natural form of dramatic language: while the verse form is not natural, as it is circumscribed by the rules of prosody. No doubt, the introduction here and there, of a few poetical pieces, as good as prose and better adapted to convey the meaning, enhances the gracefulness of composition; and for this reason, poets might very well introduce, in proper places, verses of the kind above described. Further, sometimes the exquisite metrical form even makes up for what is wanting in words and sense; prose on the other hand has to be imparted an elegance by the excellence of the graceful arrangement of choice words and ideas; hence it is that prose composition is considered to be more difficult. Thus in the *Kavyalankara*, while commenting on the Sutra,

"काव्यं गद्यं पद्यं च"

Vamana says:—

"गद्यस्य पूर्वं निर्देशो दुर्लक्षविषयत्वेन दुर्बन्धत्वात् ।"

and cites as authority for his position the saying of a learned writer who had acquired a reputation during his time,

"गद्यं कवीनां निकषं वदन्ति ।"

Hence it follows that, in *Natakas*, prose is the chief factor, while verse is not so important. When prose attains elegance in words and sense, then does the *Rupaka* serve its end. For this reason, *Bhasa* mostly employes in his writings short bits of prose highly charming in sense and expression; and the poetical pieces he uses, are similar in form to the prose ones, and they are employed occasionally. Therefore it is that he constructs sometimes acts in his *Natakas* with not a line of verse, for example the 2nd and 3rd acts of *Svapnanataka* and the 2nd act of the *Charudatta*. The *Rasa* conveyed is exhibited with a completeness which is merely due to the weaving of the prose pieces expressing the *Rasa*. If the *Pancharatra* contains a large portion of verse, it is in point of lucidity not dissimilar to prose. Although *Kalidasa* has followed *Bhasa* in his *Sakuntala* in all ways, yet he has not been able to impress on his prose, the stamp of exquisiteness that marks the prose of *Bhasa*.

The reason for this is not far to seek. Certainly in *Bhasa's* time, the Sanskrit language, like other spoken languages of the time, had so wide a range in the varied transactions of daily life, that the poets of the time commanded a wealth of words elegant and well-suited to graphically depict their ideas. The true and essential nature of things revealed itself to the poets of the time. Hence was *Bhasa* able to compose without any effort short easy prose pieces enriched with lofty ideas. During *Kalidasa's* time, on the other hand, Sanskrit had so far strayed away from the path of spoken languages, that words similar to those above described had to be sought after, and the poets were unable to form original ideas as they generally followed the ideas of others. It is on this account that in *Kalidasa's* time new *Kavyas* were considered neither good nor viewed with favour and regard. This fact can be inferred from the following passage of the *Malavikagnimitra*:-

*"पुराणमित्येव न साधु सर्वं नचापि काव्यं नवमित्यवद्यम् ।"

"वर्तमानकवेः कालिदासस्य क्रियायां कथं बहुमानः ।"

From the following words of *Bhamaha*,

"मुख्यस्तावदयं न्यायो यत् स्वशक्त्या प्रवर्तते ।

अन्ये सारस्वता नाम सन्त्यन्योक्तानुवादिनः ॥"

it will be seen that even in *Bhamaha's* time, the poets used to depend on other writers, not to speak of later times. It is therefore clear why the beauty of the conversational prose which shines in *Bhasa's* writings is not found in the *Sakuntala*. But the renowned poet *Kalidasa* ambitious of winning reputation as an author of good poetical compositions, at a time when new good poetical works were deplorably scarce, followed with great effort the old track left by the archaic writers, *Valmiki*, *Vyasa* and *Bhasa*, and being a genius gifted with bright conceptions, began to write new poetical works (*Kavyas*) embellished with a wealth of vivid images and excellence, well worth imitation by all succeeding poets and at

* Vide Appendix II (c).

the same time governed himself by the rules of *Panini* and *Bhamaha*. The sweetness of verse which obtains in the *Raghuvamsa* and other kindred *Kavyas* is enshrined also in the *Sakuntala* in a similar or even a greater degree, while a natural grace of diction and exquisiteness of ideas pre-eminently prevails in all his slokas to a degree which is not far short of that of the compositions of the archaic writers.

15. Meeting the contention that Kalidasa lived not long after Bhasa.

It must not be argued on account of the prevalence of this naturalness of grace, that *Kalidasa* succeeded *Bhasa* only within a short interval of time, for it stands to reason that, although *Kalidasa* came into existence centuries after *Bhasa*, yet impelled by a desire to imitate the writings of ancient authors, he was able to infuse into his writings an archaic poetic flavour, not quite distinguishable from that of the ancient writings. If it is not now impossible even for a poet of the modern times, bent on imitating ancient writings, to instil into his productions an archaic flavour, it should much less be impossible to *Kalidasa* who has overtopped the entire community of suceeding poets by his marvellous poetic genius.

16. The similarity of Prakrit in Bhasa and Kalidasa.

Nor from the fact that there is a close similarity between the Prakrit of *Kalidasa* and that of *Bhasa*, can it be inferred that the interval between the age of *Bhasa* and that of *Kalidasa* should measure only a brief space of time. As already mentioned, when Sanskrit left the conversational arena, Prakrit which followed on the heels of Sankrit shared the same fate, and as such, the Prakrit at the time of *Kalidasa* had necessarily to conform itself to the Prakrit of *Bhasa's* time, for Prakrit being no longer a spoken dialect, could undergo no change. Since *Kalidasa* had of necessity to use Prakrit in his dramas, and as no change had taken place in that dialect, his Prakrit must necessarily be similar in character to that of the ancient *Natakas*; and even to this day, in writing new *Natakas* poets still follow the customary practice of using the Prakrit of the kind above described. Thus, as the observance of a resemblance between the Prakrit used in a modern dramatical composition and the Prakrit of *Kalidasa* could never go to establish that its writer should have lived closely after *Kalidasa*, in the same way the observance in *Kalidasa's Natakas* of the Prakrit similar to that found in *Bhasa*, could not justify the inference that *Kalidasa* should have come into existence within a short interval of time after *Bhasa*. *

---

* Accepting the priority of Bhasa to Chanakya, Mahamahopadhyaya Haraprasada Sastri M. A. C. I. E. of Calcutta, thus explains the modern look of the Prakrit of Bhasa in a letter of his addressed to me:—The king of Aryavarta between the mountains Himalays and Vindhyas and between the two seas mentioned in the Bharatavakya is, I believe, one of the Nandas. Perhaps you will remember that some three years ago I wrote a paper on the origin of 'Indian Drama' in the Journal of our Society throwing out a suggestion that the Bharatanatyasastra published in the Kavyamala Series was perhaps composed in the 2nd century B. C. because the Parthians there are called Pathravas and not Pallavas as in Manu and other later works.

I find that Bhasa disregards altogether the rules of dramturgy laid down in that work. I also pointed out in that paper that, before the compilation of that work, there were several schools of dramaturgy. and Bhasa perhaps belonged to one of the older schools of dramaturgy and therefore he was not aware of the rules laid down in the Natyasastra.

I have got a curious confirmation of the existence of the dramaturgy in ancient India in the fact that Kautalya has classed Kusilavas or actors with the Sudras. Natyasastra says that the original Kusilavas were all Brahmins or better still of divine origin, but they ridiculed the Rishis and therefore they were cursed to become Sudras, So their Sudra-hood is later than the origin of the drama. As in Chanakya's time they were classed to be Sudras, we are to infer that at that time drama was an old, old institution.

There is one strong point in favour of a later date for Bhasa and that is his Prakrit. It is not so old as 4th or 5th century B. C. but anyone who has studied the dramatic Prakrit carefully knows fully well that the copyists always changed the Prakrit of their authors into the Prakrit current in their own time. And that is why Bhasa's Prakrit has a modern look. But there is one point which is never used by later poets but which is found only in old Pali works which shows its antiquity and that word is "Ama" for Yes.

Further, as language adapts itself to the course of conversational thought, its vocabulary also undergoes a consequent change. When it ceases to be spoken, the forms of words in the language are no longer affected or changed.

17. Sanskrit has ceased to be a spoken dialect at the time of Kalidasa.

But it might be asked how it is assumed that Sanskrit ceased to be a spoken language in *Kalidasa's* time, as also Prakrit. In this connection, it may be premised that language has three gradual stages: the first is that in which it is freely employed in conversation from infancy; the second stage is attained when it is written as well as spoken; and the third is reached when it ceases to be a spoken language, but is merely employed in writings. The utility of grammar is twofold: one is to easily explain the forms and derivation of words current in the language; and the other is to keep them from undergoing modifications in form due to carelessness, ignorance or incapacity, as well as to prevent the entry of new words into the language. The second may be included in the first; for such changes in form and the new words that may be introduced, not falling within the scope of its rules, grammar, by ignoring them, reveals their inacceptability, while it explains the established words. In the first two stages of the growth of a language, when the current of discourse in daily life flows unimpeded, the works on grammar prevalent at the time, can neither arrest the mutation of forms taking place in words nor prevent the introduction of new words; for, as grammar is merely confined to the explanation of words which have at the time become established at the various walks of life, it could not become applicable to words which may subsequently become established in the current speech of the times posterior to its appearance. For this reason, new grammatical works adapting themselves to the course of speech of the times are then and there composed It therefore follows that no grammar attains a final stage so long as the language to which it pertains has not emerged from the second stage. The language which has not departed from the current of conversational thought cannot become defined or settled in its form owing to the possibility of the subsequent formal modification and the introduction of new words. But when a language ceases to be spoken, i. e., when the causes of formal modifications and influx of fresh words cease to operate, necessarily it has reached its final and settled stage. It should therefore be understood that the grammar of a language, that has attained its final stage, is also settled and fixed; and the grammar which is applicable to a language, which has not reached that final stage, remains still undeveloped. Thus in a series of successive grammatical productions, that treatise, after the appearance of which the language to which it relates ceases to be spoken but is employed merely in literary compositions, can be deemed as completely developed; for, on the decline of the current of speech, which is the cause for the developement, there is no scope for entertaining any apprehension as to any future change occurring in the forms of words. As a matter of fact such a grammar has to be viewed in the way in which settled mandatory precepts are usually viewed. This is the fact.

18. At the time of the Mahabhashya, Sanskrit had ceased to be a spoken language.

The author of the Mahabhashya evidently considers the *Paniniya Vyakarana* as a settled grammar of the Sanskrit language; for he regards only the words recognised by it as pure and acceptable, and all others as unacceptable, and enjoins the use of those pure words as meritorious and denounces the uses of other words as sacrelegious; and these directions have been scrupulously and reverently followed by all men.

If he were to consider it otherwise (that the Sanskrit had not then ceased to be a spoken language) he would not have made a sweeping and general pronouncement of unworthiness with respect to words not recognised by *Panini*, for such a pronouncement would amount to the statement that even all the formal changes that must necessarily be brought in by the strong course of current speech in the language are unworthy, and would amount in effect only to this instruction, that the speakers of the language should so withstand the irresistable course of speech that it might not give rise to any such mutation of forms, or even if such changes take place, they should not be allowed to enter into the language. And this would be quite inconsistent with the views of such revered personages who naturally wish for the growth of the language. Even if desired, the people could not fight against discourse when it remains unimpeded. Therefore it must thus be assumed:—that the author of the *Mahabhashya* found that, in his time, the Sanskrit language was mostly gone out of the current of ordinary speech owing to the prevalence in the country of several other languages in different stages of development. With no expectation regarding the growth of the language in later times, and fearing that it would gradually fade away in course of time, he conceived the idea of so protecting the language that it might on no account leave even the stage of being employed in written compositions. Considering that, when people at large should, with the help of this Vyakarana, gain a grounding in the language from the Sanskrit works current at the time, and when they should happen to write new works, the Sanskrit language would safely hold fast to the stage of being embodied in written compositions, the author of the *Mahabhashga*, with the desire of instilling into the minds of the readers a respect for the grasp and use of sound words, attributed merit to them on the authority of valuable texts. The people also following the said advice entertain to the present day that profound regard, which is commonly paid to the precepts of the vedic texts, towards *Panini's* precepts which are characterised by a gravity due to their furnishing immense help in explaining words which form the groundwork in the building up of all Sanskrit compositions. So far is therefore plain, that even during the age of the author of the *Mahabkashya* Sanskrit had ceased to be a spoken language, not to speak of the time of *Kalidasa*.

19. Prakrit had ceased to be a spoken dialect at the time of Kalidasa.

The quesstion how Prakrit ceased to be employed in conversational speech has now to be answered. It can be urged that, when Sanskrit ceased to be a spoken language, Prakrit which was developing side by side with it, also shared a similar fate. How Prakrit came to develop itself side by side with the Sanskrit language, may now be enquired. In this connection the sequence of the origin of Sanskrit and of Prakrit may be considered. Although there is a school of thought which has gained favour with orthodox scholars, that Sanskrit must be regarded as eternal (having no origin) on account of the fact that Sanskrit words are embodied in the Vedas which are eternal, still if it is to be inferred that in virtue of its being a language not different from the other languages it should also have sprung up with an origin and gradually developed, then there is a royal road leading to the inference.

20. The origin of Sanskrit.

In ancient times, there was some unknown language current among the people, which they employed for the purpose of communicating their ideas among themselves, in respect of their sheer physical requirements. In the gradual development of the conversational faculty of the people, it began to spread, and whenever the intelligent among the people began to discover, by their own efforts, new things, one after another, both spiritual and material, capable of being employed or discarded, and also to found new schools of thought, and when they evinced a desire to make their fellowmen and those who would be born after them, acquainted with the results of their labour and the means of discovering such objects and developing their form, quality and utility, then in the same language they began to compose works on these subjects. Thus by a series of successive generations of men gifted with intelligence, a series of discoveries of novel objects and consequently a series of successive new works treating of the attainment of the said objects, began to come into existence and gradually became widespread. While the state of composition stood thus, a multiplicity of refinements had entered into the language, which would never have been the case if the language had remained merely a spoken tongue. In the written compositions again, no pains were spared to convey the maximum of thoughts in the minimum of words to avoid their repetition, to choose appropriate and happy words and to arrange them gracefully. As new thoughts were successfully born of the more intelligent heads, new words too came in thousands into the language. Elegant styles of exposition also adorned the language. Thus blending together the literary compositions and the oral speech, each of which helped the development of the other, a certain branch of the original tongue gradually attained the highest refinement in all the words, which branch was the one embraced by the intelligent community above spoken of, their descendant and those that looked up to them for guidance and direction. And this, I think, is called 'Samskrita,' (the refined) from the refinements secured to it by the steadily continued efforts of generations of intelligent heads. Of the generality of the people of those days, such of them as were poor in intellect or did not take care to be guided by the more intellectual of them, carried on their discourses in the original language itself, in which there began to spring up many new words which are the natural outcome of the spread of their discourses in daily life and many excellences due to the acquaintance with the Samskrita-speaking people; and these developed by gradual degrees. Thus from the original root-language, some non-Sanskrit branches also sprang up. The Sanskrit, on account of the sterling nature of its refinement it had undergone, and on account of the settled nature of the written works studied by those desirous of cultivating its knowledge, came to be spoken in the different countries without any change in its form. The other branch languages not being favoured by the two facts above mentioned, came to be spoken in different forms in different countries and to derive their ideas from Sanskrit itself. Hence Sanskrit was viewed as a model by other non-Sanskrit languages in all manner of ways in respect of words and in respect of sense, and came to be regarded as the nourisher of the said languages, and by virtue of this characteristic, it ever deserves to be styled as the "Mother" of the said languages. Thus must have been the probable branching of the original root-language.

21. The origin of Prakrit.

Another kind of language was prevalent which must necessarily have come into existence during the times when Sanskrit was wielding undisputed sway in the field of speech. Sanskrit was spoken well by men well educated in it, and with some slight difference by those less educated in it, but never well by men who were not taught in it. Women also mostly by their want of training in the language were not able to pronounce the Sanskrit words in the proper manner, as also children. Hence in the tongue of the illiterate, Sanskrit came to be pronounced in a slightly or largely modified form according to the difference of their relative want of capacity. This modified or rather mutilated form of Sanskrit is called Prakrit on account of its being derived from Sanskrit, its 'Prakriti' or origin. This Prakrit which was spoken by the uneducated men and women of all castes, on account of the contact with the discourses carried on by the educated people of the four castes, did not undergo very great modifications, and as such, is the best of its kind. That which was spoken by the men and women outside the pale of the four castes who were not moving with educated classes, was much more corrupted on account of their little acquaintance with the educated, and greater acquaintance with those who were speaking the best kind of Prakrit referred to above, and on account of the contact with those who were speaking non-Sanskrit off-shoots of the original root-langage mentioned above. For this reason, this Prakrit is not pure. This again became probably subdivided into several branches on account of the difference in proportion of the changes undergone to a large extent which compared with Prakrit in the purest form, and on account of their being derived from Prakrit, their origin. These are explained in the grammatical works on Prakrit.* Thus with the spread of Sanskrit as a spoken language, it must necessarily be taken that Prakrit also developed side by side with it, in the field of speech, adapting itself to Sanskrit so closely as if it were the shadow of the other. Such being the case, it should be understood, that when the current of discourse in the Sanskrit language declined, the current of discourse in the

* See Appendix II, (D)

Prakrit also declined, and following the fate which overtook the original Sanskrit, its shadow Prakrit also departed from the field of spoken languages. When the Sanskrit-speaking people evinced a desire to entertain themselves with the art of dramatic performances, they began to construct dramatical compositions suited to their tastes As the language of the actors in the Rupakas had naturally to conform itself to that in daily life, that Prakrit which was commonly employed by women and others in their respective discourses in life, came to be used by them in the Rupakas as well. As to the fact that people diverted themselves with enjoying dramatic performances during the times when Sanskrit was the spoken language, no doubt need be entertained; for, from the two sutras of *Panini*,

'पाराशर्यशिलालिभ्यां भिक्षुनटसूत्रयोः' (4-3-100)

'कर्मन्दकृशाश्वादिनिः' (4-3-111)

which refer to the scientific treatises on the art of acting, it is plain that the art of acting treated of should necessarily have been in existence much earlier. This period when the art of acting was in vogue prior to *Panini* must be beyond doubt that during which the Sanskrit language was a spoken one.

22. The language of Asoka's time.

The language employed in the edicts of Asoka or Pali might well be one of the non-Sanskrit offshoots of the original root language aforesaid. The language was in ancient times spoken by a number of people, and when the majority of them embraced the Buddhist religion, it was adopted in the Buddhistic literature. When some of the Sanskrit-speaking and Prakrit-speaking people professed Buddhism and intermingled with those who had already been Buddhists, then an irregular admixture of Sanskrit and Prakrit with the said language took place. Further the speakers of the said language began to introduce deliberately into it an admixture of Sanskrit on account of its capacity to impart a peculiar grace to the language, just as it is done in Telugu, Malayalam and other vernaculars. Therefore it is but proper that it should consist of a large proportion of Sanskrit and possess a similarity to Prakrit; and neither is it Prakrit itself, nor Prakrit in its earlier form, nor Prakrit in its later stage, but quite a different dialect from Prakrit. Only on account of its resemblance to Prakrit could the term Prakrit be applied to it. Be it as it may, whether it was spoken in Asoka's times or whether it was employed merely in the Buddhistic writings, certainly it commanded a high respect at the hands of the Buddhists of the time. It might also well be that even during the time following that of Asoka, the said language was, by some Buddhist poet, either attracted by a love of the language or out of mere curiosity fancifully employed along with Sanskrit in some dramatic compositions of his own. In any way in the Rupakas written by poets who kept abreast of the current of the Sanskrit tongue in speech and writing, only that Prakrit which is counterpart of Sanskrit, as already explained, should have been employed along with Sanskrit. It should not be forgotten that the same method was, as already stated, followed by the poets who lived at the time of the decline of Sanskrit as a spoken language.

Some people may surmise that at the time of *Kalidasa*, Sanskrit had ceased to be a spoken tongue; but Prakrit has stepped in as the spoken dialect, and that *Kalidasa*, wishing to make his characters speak in conformity to the form of discourse then prevalent, used this spoken Prakrit as the Prakrit of the female and similar characters. If it were so, he should have, Prakrit being the only spoken tongue, made kings and similar characters also speak in some Prakrit different from that of the female and similar characters, and not in Sanskrit. But to suppose that he should have adopted the form of speech then prevalent only in the case of female characters, is irrelevent. Thus, that *Kalidasa* has followed the settled practice with regard to the form of speech of the various characters both male and female, is due to his desire to tread the path well trodden by ancient poets, and not to any attempt to make each of his characters speak severally of the same tongue spoken in the world in *Kalidasa's* time.

23. Bhasa's priority to Panini

It has now to be considered whether the archaic (आर्ष) words of *Bhasa* referred to above were used by him (i) before *Panini's* time or (ii) during the time of *Panini* himself, or (iii) after *Panini's* grammar came into existence and before it gained any publicity, or lastly (iv) after the grammar had gained publicity. The fourth of these positions cannot stand in any case for this reason that a poet would not dare to employ words which are opposed to the precepts of *Panini*, when they are known to be Apasabdas (अपशब्दा:); since, the Kavyas being the embodiment of words, would become, if they contain Apasabdas, as repulsive as a body afflicted by leprosy; and when such incorrect words are heedlessly used in written compositions, they would never commend themselves to enlightened scholars. If they do not win the favor of enlightened scholars, how could the public cherish any liking for them, and still more, how could the poet attain any reputation when it depends on popular opinion? On the contrary, he could be treated with derision by the public, and, if he is a believer in the Sastra which pronounces sin on the authors of incorrect expressions, he would also incur that odium. In the case of *Bhasa*, on the other hand, his *natakas*, though replete with such usages, have been highly extolled even by such votaries of *Panini* as *Kalidasa*, and his fame again has reached its farthest limit.

The third of these above positions cannot stand either.

24. Publicity of Panini's Anusasana.

When could that period be when *Panini's* *Anusasana* had not gained publicity? It could not be the first century before Christ for the *Mahabhashya* had then come into existence, and as such, Panini's grammar together with the *Mahabhashya* must have been at its zenith of reputation; and further we are going to prove that it had a wide currency in the 2nd century B. C. also. Nor could it be the 2nd century B. C. when the *Mahabhashya*, according to some enquirers into ancient history, was composed. For, that Panini's grammar was popular even then, is evident from the words of *Bhartrihari* (भर्तृहरि) when he says in his *Vakyapadiya* that the *Sangraha*, a bulky work of *Vyadi* on *Panini's* school of Vyakarana, having got obsolete, as the students from ignorance liked to have brief treatises, *Patanjali* wrote his *Mahabhashya* summarising the substance of the *Sangraha*. If *Panini's* grammar had not then been prevalent, *Bhartrihari* would have attributed its decline to the general dislike.

Bhartrihari's words run thus :-

"प्रायेण संक्षेपरुचीनल्पविद्यापरिग्रहान् ।
संप्राप्य वैयाकरण न् सङ्ग्रहेऽस्तमुपागते ॥ ४८४ ॥
कृतेऽथ पतञ्जलिना गुरुणा तीर्थदर्शिना ।
सर्वेषां न्यायबीजानां महाभाष्ये निबन्धने ॥ ४८५ ॥
अलब्धगाधे गाम्भीर्यादुत्तान इव सौष्ठवात् ॥"

(वाक्यपदी० काण्ड० २)

Of these, the first couplet has been thus commented on by *Punya-Raja*:-

"इह पुरा पाणिनीयेऽस्मिन् व्याकरणे व्याड्युपरचितं ग्रन्थलक्षपरिमाणं संग्रहाभिधानं निबन्धनमासीत् । तच्च कालवशात् सुकुमारबुद्धीन् वैयाकरणान् प्राप्यास्तमुपगतम् । तस्मात् क्लेशभीरुत्वात् संक्षेपरुचयस्ते जनाः । अत एवाल्पो विद्यासु परिग्रहः स्वीकारो येषां ते तथा । ततस्तैः संग्रहाध्ययन उपेक्षिते सत्यस्तं यातः संग्रहः ।"

and he also observes, commenting on the last of the above lines thus:-

"एतेन संग्रहानुसारेण भगवता पतञ्जलिना संग्रहसंक्षेपभूतमेव प्रायशो भाष्यमुपनिबद्धमित्युक्तं वेदितव्यम् ।"

It therefore follows that it cannot be the third or even the 4th century B. C. for this reason, that as some period of time has to be fixed to indicate the interval which should reasonably have elapsed for the *Sangraha's* getting an ascendency over men's minds and for its subsequent falling into disfavour, at the least a period of these two centuries should be assigned, and during this period *Panini's* grammar must necessarily have been in wide circulation. It has therefore to be surmised that the period in question must be the fifth century B. C. The first half at least of this century must denote the time of *Katyayana*, for it stands to reason that the author of the short sutra-like composition called *Vartika*, must necessarily have preceded *Vyadi*, the author of the extensive treatise. And the grammar of *Panini* must have been in vogue even then, for the author of *Vartika* expanded *Panini's* grammar and filled up the portions which *Panini* had left out on account of oversight or on account of the springing up of new words after the time of *Panini*, by composing new rules adapted to the discourse of the times, for improving the knowledge of the students of grammar. Thus the period, in which *Panini's* grammar had not gained publicity, may therefore be the second half of the fifth century B. C. or the first half of the sixth century B. C. As this must denote the latest age that could be assigned to *Panini*, our discussion necessarily leads us to a consideration of the second of the four positions started with. The second position also cannot stand; for, as *Panini* considers certain words as sound and *Bhasa* certain others sound, if both were contemporaneous, it would be highly inconsistent that such difference of views should exist between them, both of them being close followers of the current tongue. Hence the enquiry leads us to accept the remaining one—the first of the above positions. If these words, which have been accepted as archaic (आर्ष) had got firmly rooted in the discourses in times previous to *Panini*, then, these, being the ordinary (लौकिक) usages, should have necessarily been brought by *Panini* under his precepts which conform to the ordinary usages; and that, as a matter of fact, the words have not been treated of by him, lands us in a dilemma. The way to get out of this difficulty will be furnished by the answer to the question, how it happened that even the archaic usages found in the writings of *Vyasa* and others, which were also in use in common parlance without being regarded differently from the ordinary, have also not been treated of by *Panini*. If it is explained that these usages, being merely confined to the discourses among the Rishis, could not be regarded as ordinary ones, while only words distinguishable from them have been regarded as ordinary ones by *Panini*, and as such, the archaic usages, neither pertaining to the people nor embodied in vedic utterances, have not been treated of by *Panini*, then the same would hold good in the present case also. Let us take that, considering these usages as being included in the vedic usages,

Panini has certainly brought them within the scope of the precepts pertaining to the vedic usages, as he has used the word Arsha (आर्ष) instead of Vaidika (वैदिक) in his Sutra.

" सम्बुद्धौ शाकल्यस्येतावनार्षे " (1-1-16)

thereby indicating that the precepts pertaining to the Vedic words are also applicable to Arsha words, and as the author of the *Mahabhashya* also says,

" छन्दोवदृषयः कुर्वन्ति ", छन्दोवत् कवयः कुर्वन्ति "

that is, Rishis and venerable poets are accustomed to use words like vedic usages, then this would equally apply to solve the previous question also. Hence the first position, i.e., that the archaic usages found in the works of *Bhasa* were employed by him only before *Panini's* times, holds good now. In this connection, it must be conceded that even in times much anterior to *Panini*, there were dramatic compositions written, read and enacted, for *Panini* refers to the *Natasutras* (Histrionic rules) of the Munis, *Silali* and *Krisasva*, thus indicative of the prior existence of the dramatical art itself, in his sutras,

" पाराशर्यशिलालिभ्यां भिक्षुनटसूत्रयोः " (4-3-110)

" कर्मन्दकृशाश्वादिनिः " (4-3-111)

These *Natasutras* presuppose the existence of dramatical compositions to which they are applicable as the scientific canons of an art could come into existence only after the art itself. As these dramatical compositions have commanded the respect of the Munis, they must have been composed by the Munis and must be archaic in their manner. Since such are *Bhasa's Natakas*, they may reasonably be regarded as the dramatic compositions referred to.

25. The popularity of the epic of Rama in fourth century B. C.

If the age of *Bhasa* be fixed at the fifth or sixth century B. C., then it would be inconsistent that he should have written the *Abhisheka-nataka* and *Pratimanataka* on the materials pertaining to *Sri Rama's* life, as the epic describing *Rama's* life and doings (or the *Ramayana*) has not been dated before the second century B. C. This is not so, for it has not been conclusively established that the *Ramayana* was not written before the second century B. C. Further, from the fact that *Chanakya* whose age has been fixed as the fourth century B. C. refers as authority to the story of Rama, it must have been largely in vogue even before the fourth century B. C. The said reference occurs in the *Arthasastra* of *Kautalya*, in discussing the fate of former princes who had not curbed their senses:-

"मानाद् रावणः परदारानप्रयच्छन् (विननाश)
दुर्योधनश्च राज्यादंशम्" (कौटल्य० 1-5-3.)

Here it is described that *Ravana* was killed for not having restored another's wife, and *Duryodhana*, for not having made over a portion of the kingdom. By the destruction of *Ravana* the epic of *Rama*, and by the destruction of *Duryodyana*, the epic of *Yudhishthira* are referred to in the above, and these two epics are undoubtedly the *Ramayana* and *Mahabharata*. The two works as they are referred to as authorities by *Chanakya* could not possibly have been written at his own time or even a little earlier, but must necessarily have been composed some seven or eight centuries before him. As the matter stands thus, there is no reason to doubt the popularity of *Ramayana* at the time of *Bhasa*. As a matter of fact, however, by the sequence of the description of the incidents about *Ravana* and *Duryodhana*, *Chanakaya* has referred to the established opinion of the people of his time, that *Ramayana* is the earlier of the two; and as-such, it is reasonable that *Ramayana* must necessarily have come into existence even before the *Mahabharata*. The narration of the story of *Ramayana*, the reference in many places to *Hanuman* and others contained therein and the description of *Rama* as an *Avatara* of Vishnu, all these found in the *Mahabharata* are consistent with the above inference.

Apart from these, there is a view that the epic of *Rama* is anterior to the time of *Chanakya*, and that this very same epic being subsequently enlarged by the introduction of a variety of new materials has become the *Ramayna* of the present day. If the portion ascribing divinity as an avatara of Vishnu to *Sri Rama* found in it, is to be considered as a subsequent interpolation then it could not hold good ; for the surmise that the current *Ramayana* is an enlargement made by later writers, is not grounded on a solid basis. Or even if there were any interpolation, on account of the fact that it would not be probable that, unless *Rama* is described as an avatara of Vishnu even to the slightest extent, in the previous epic of Rama, it would find a place in the later *Ramayana*, the portion ascribing divinity to *Rama* could not be properly considered as a later interpolation. The belief that *Rama* is God Vishnu himself, that his doings themselves are divine, and that on account of its embodying his life and deeds, the study of the *Ramayana* leads to the acquisition of Punya or merit, has firmly rooted itself in the minds of the people among successive generations of the pious, in respect of the current *Ramayana*. Hence the suggestion that the original *Ramayana* did not embody the divine attribute of *Rama*, and that it was by chance subsequently implanted in the later *Ramayana* and given a prominence therein will not be convincing ; for, which man of reason would consider divine a hero whom he had till then been viewing as human from a certain epic, for the reason, that in a later epic based on it the same hero is depicted as divine. Thus it becomes established that even before the time of *Chanakya* the divinity of *Sri Rama* has acquired firm ground in the epic of *Rama*.

26. Rama an Avatara of Vishnu.

Bhasa evidently knew the Sakya mendicants, for he makes mention of *Sramana* in * *Pratijna*, *Avimaraka* and *Charudatta*. Merely on this account, it is not possible to infer that *Bhasa's* age should be posterior to that of Buddha, for it is

27. Reference to Sramana.

* Vide Pratijna, Act 3, Avimaraka, Act 5, and Charudatta, Act 3.

well nigh possible that *Sakya Sramanas* should have existed even prior to the time of Buddha. There is nothing to render it impossible to infer that a form of religious observance, which had taken root in times before Buddha, and which was in vogue among the Sakyas though in its infancy, was established on a firmer basis by the sage Buddha, sprung from the race of the Sakyas. Tapasvins (तपस्विनः) were styled *Sramanas* either on account of their laborious penance or on account of their training their bodies in the practice of religious rituals. Thus in such Brahmanic treatises as *Vaikhanasa-dharmaprasna* and others, the term *Sramana* is employed mostly as synonymous with one practising religious austerities. Thus the term *Sakya Saramanas* designate those among the *Sakyas* who adhere to the practice of religious austerities. When the term *Sramana* came as a rule to be appropriated by the Buddhists, whose tenets are opposed to those of the vedic observants, to designate their own mendicants, it ceased to be adopted by the vedic people with regard to their own mendicants.

28. Chanakya.

Thus *Bhasa's* age, fixed in the introduction of the *Svapna-vasavadatta* as being anterior to that of *Chanakya*, the author of the *Artha-Sastra*, becomes now more firmly established. That *Chanakya* is the author of the present *Artha-Sastra*, should not even for a moment be doubted, for the reason that it is expressly mentioned therein that **Chanakya* himself composed the treatise and that it is not stated therein that it was composed by any of his disciples. Besides, an archaic style, found in the passage of the *Artha-Sastra*, is sufficient by itself to generate a firm belief in the readers, regarding its authorship by *Chanakya*.

---

* Vide Appendix II (e).

It is seen that these natakas of *Bhasa* do not follow the rules of the dramatic compositions described in the *Natyasastra* of the present day, whose authorship has been traditionally ascribed to the sage *Bharata* (an incomplete copy of the commentary of which, written by *Abhinavaguptacharya*, is in our possession). Of these *Natakas*, the *Svapnavasavadatta*, the *Balacharita*, the *Avimaraka*, the *Abhishekanataka* and the *Pratimanataka* might, on account of their consisting of not less than five acts and other characteristics, be considered as *Natakas* *; the *Pancharatra*, owing to the fact that it consists of nearly a dozen actors and of three acts, each succeeding act being shorter in extent than the one going before, may be reckoned as *Samavakara*, but the Rasa running through it is not Sringara and each of the actors therein delineated does not serve a different purpose, which facts are the essence of *Samavakara*; the *Madhyamavyayoga*, *Dutavakya*, *Dutaghatotkacha* and *Karnabhara* can be reckoned amongst *Vyayogas* on account of their embodying a large number of male characters and of being made up of single act, but the fewness of the female characters which is also required in a *Vyayoga* is not found in the *Dutavakya* and *Karnabhara*; the *Urubhanga* might be considered as an *Utsrishtikanka* on account of the Karunarasa and on account of the lamentation of the female characters, but the lamentation is not largely protrayed. The *Pratijnanatika* may be treated as an *Ihamriga* on account of its consisting of four acts and on account of its depicting the battle as brought about by women, but it has been described in the colophon as a *Natika*; again the *Charudatta* is incomplete, yet it can be treated to be in the same footing as the *Mrichchhakatika*; but in *Balacharita* an actual battle takes place, and in the *Abhishekanataka* an actual death is represented. As these two have been forbidden by the rules pertaining to the *Natya-Sastra*, the transgression here of the rules laid down therein

29. Bhasa's priority to the current Natyasastra.

---

* Vide definitions of nataka, nati, Samavakara etc. in chapter 18 of the Natya Veda.

is explicit. The mention of the name of the author is prescribed by the *Natyasastra* *; that too has not been done in the case of any of these Rupakas; thus the transgression of the requisites prescribed in the *Natyasastra* is everywhere plainly seen. This much therefore can be concluded that there must have been in existence in the times of *Bhasa* a certain other *Natyasastra* consistent with the nature of *Bhasa's natakas*. This might be the *Natasutra* ‡ referred to by *Panini* as composed by *Silalimuni* or by *Krisasvamuni*; or this might be a certain other old *Natyasastra* written by *Bharatamuni* himself, as is seen from the fact that the name of *Bharata* is mentioned by *Bhasa* in the term "*Bharatavakya*".

30. The current Natyasastra an enlarged form of the ancient one.

The *Natyasastra* mentioned above, which is current in the literature of the present bay, might be a rescension of the original *Natyasastras* of *Bharata* and others, compiled by later writers, so as to suit the dramatical works subsequently composed; and it may be that, on account of its embodying to a greater extent the dramatic principles of *Bharata*, it has been published as having been composed by *Bharatamuni*. That the *Natyasastra*, which is followed in the dramatic literature of the present day, is a later compilation, and that it came into existence in about the second century B. C., have conclusively been established by Mahamahopadhyaya Haraprasada Sastri M. A., C. I. E., in the Journal and Proceedings of the Royal Asiatic Society of Bengal (N. S.), Vol. V, No. 9, of October 1909, PP. 351-361. The words *Aryaputra*, *Bhadramuka*, *Kumara* and others prescribed in the current *Natyasastra* (vide 17th Adhyaya) to be used by the dramatic characters in respect of particular persons, were

* 'प्रसाद्य रङ्गं विधिवत् कवेर्नाम च कीर्तयेत् ।' (भरतनाट्य॰ अध्या॰5 श्लो॰154)

‡ 'पाराशर्यशिलालिभ्यां भिक्षुनटसूत्रयोः' (4-3-110)
'कर्मन्दकृशाश्वादिनिः' (4-3-111)

found employed in the *Natakas* before, and are therefore adopted among the canons of dramaturgy by the compilers of the *Natyasastra*. Of these terms, *Aryaputra*, *Bhadramuka*, *Kumara* and some others, are found in the *Natakas* of *Bhasa*, and certain others might have been emyloyed in other archaic dramatic compositions. In the *Svapnanataka*, the term *Aryaputra* is employed as a word of respect by the chamberlain of *Vasavadatta's* father in addressing King *Udayana*. This form of address, which should be employed only by *Vasavadatta* in addressing *Udayana*, her lord, was complimentarily adopted by her father's chamberlain with a view to bring out the affection cherished by the chamberlain towards *Vasavadatta*. In the same manner the form of address adopted by the servant of *Ugrasena* towardes *Vasudeva* i. e., styling him *Aryaputra*, occurring in the *Balacharita*, is employed as a mark of respect out of regard for *Devaki*.

31. No patron of Bhasa suggested by the plays.

It is not possible to make out from the *Natakas* of *Bhasa* whether he was patronised by any particular king; nor had he a desire even to mention the name of any such king. For, if he had desired to do so, he could very well have mentioned his name either in the *Sthapana* or in the *Bharatavakya* in its proper connection. Even though the name of the patron prince is not mentioned in the *Sthapana* itself, inasmuch as he had not mentioned even his own name, then in the *Bharatavakya* it should necessarily be mentioned. The name, only when explicitly mentioned, will be recognised by the readers as the name of a particular king, a way thus being made for perpetuating his name. The patron king also having known the services of the poet in immortalising his name will extend his favours towards him.

The term *Rajasimha* occurring in the *Bharatavakya* "राजसिंहः प्रशास्तु नः" could not point to any particular king, for if it were to denote the name of any particular king, the kingly relation of the king to the poet who prays for the king's prosperity would not be expressed by the word denoting that relation, whereas in the *Bharatavakyas* "राजा भूमिं प्रशास्तु नः" (*Pratima*), "गां पातु नो नरपतिः शमितारिपक्षः" (*Urubhanga*) and "राजा राजगुणोपेतो भूमिमेकः प्रशास्तु नः" (*Karnabhara*), the above relationship is explicitly shown by the words राजा and नरपति and that it should be otherwise in the first case i. e., in that of राजसिंह, is evidently inconsistent. There was no king of repute by the name of *Rajasimha* who had lived before *Bhattabana*, *Kalidasa*, *Patanjali* and *Chanakya*. Thus it has to be concluded that the term *Rajasimha* has been employed as being synonymous with a powerful king, just like the term नृपतिसिंह in the verse "मुदितनृपतिसिंहैः" occurring in the *Karnabhara*. The hinting of the mere name of the patron king of the poet while developing the events sustaining the interest in the body of the work, elsewhere than in the *Sthapana* and the *Bharatavakya*, would be illsuited to the context and would be quite out of place and ineffective; and poets do not resort to it, for, by doing so, they would only become the subject of ridicule. Thus as the name of no particular king has been mentioned, the *Bharatavakya* appears to have been composed by *Bhasa*, with a view of invoking blessings on kings in general, so that by its being recited on the stage by future generations of dramatic actors, it could very well be made to apply equally in the case of kings who might wield the sceptre during the time that it is so recited. It is not possible to infer that the*Mrichchhakatika* was composed by *Bhasa* to gain the favour of the king *Sudraka* and published by him in the name of the latter, as may be judged by the appearance of the ideas running through the *Natakas* of *Bhasa*, in the *Mrichchhakatika* which embodies most of the passages found in the *Charudatta*. If it were so, then *Bhasa* would have destroyed his own dramatic compositions so that the reputation of his patron king as a poet might grow and that ill repute might not fall on him. As a matter of fact, the natakas of *Bhasa* have not been so destroyed by him, as is seen from the fact that *Kalidasa*, *Bhattabana* aud others have spoken about the reputation of *Bhasa* gained by means of his *Natakas*.

And it could not be said that *Bhasa* published the *Natakas* after the death of *Sudraka*. It will be monstrous to regard *Bhasa* as having deceived his royal master. Let us leave such far-fetched surmises to themselves.

32. Summary of the conclusions.

The following are the conclusions from the topics so far discussed here:—

1. that the *Svapnavasavadatta* and other *Natakas*, thirteen in number, which have been discovered, were written by one and the same poet from their close resemblance to one another in the language employed and the method of expressing the ideas;

2. that the said poet lived in times previous to the age of *Vamana*, *Dandin* and *Bhamaha*, who have quoted from these *Natakas* ad verbum, ad sensum;

3. that, from the non-mention of the name of the poet in the *Sthapana* of these *Natakas*, the said poet had lived in times before the practice of mentioning the name of the authors in their *Natakas* became customary;

(4). that, from the fact that tradition ascribes the authorship of the *Svapnavasavadatta*, one of the Rupakas in our possession, to *Bhasa*, the author of the *Svapnavasavadatta* and the other closely similar Rupakas should be *Bhasa* himself, who has been extolled by *Kalidasa*, *Bhattabana* and others;

5. that, by virtue of his writings being characterised by an intensity of *Rasa* and by a mavellously exquisite flow of language and on account of the fact that his writings are marred by an all round grace of poetical elegance common only to the archaic compositions of the sages like *Valmiki* and *Vyasa*, *Bhasa* was an archaic poet of renown and lived in times when Sanskrit was the spoken language;

6. that, on account of the fact that *Kalidasa* has imitated his writings in all ways and that he has mentioned his (*Bhasa's*) name first among the poets deserving of respect at his hands, *Bhasa* was the single poet considered by *Kalidasa* to have been endowed with high poetical excellence deserving

to be imitated by others, by virtue of his having pointed out a path to the construction of Rupakas.

7. that, bent on adapting the language and ideas of *Bhasa*, *Kalidasa*, though born considerably long after *Bhasa*, was able to exhibit, in his writings, to some extent, an exquisiteness of style, admired in the productions of *Bhasa*, and also, the similarity of the Prakrit compositions found in *Bhasa's* works is quite within the precincts of propriety;

8. that, although *Bhasa's* writings have been marked by a multiplicity of archaic usages beyond the pale of the operations of *Panini's* precepts, yet from the fact that these writings have been adopted by *Kalidasa* and others, close adherents of *Panini*, the appellation of Rishi appertained in ancient times to *Bhasa* ;

9. that, being found to disregard several of the rules found in the *Natyasastra* in his Rupakas, *Bhasa* might have followed a certain earlier *Natyasastra* referred to as *Natasutra* by *Panini*;

10. that, on account of the fact that the grammatical rules had assumed a settled form during the times of the sage *Patanjali*, in consequence of the Sanskrit ceasing to be a spoken language, *Bhasa* should have lived in an age anterior to that of the sage *Patanjali*; and from similar arguments, he should necessarily have lived long before *Katyayana* and *Panini*; and,

11. that it is quite proper that *Chanakya* quoted the verse occurring in the *Pratijna Natika* and that *Bhasa* lived considerably long before *Chanakya*.

33. Reference to Rajagriha &c.,

Thus, from the mention of *Rajagriha* in the *Svapnavasavadatta* and from the mention of *Venuvana* and *Nagavana* in the *Pratijnanatika* and from the reference to *Pataliputra* in the *Charudatta* it might be concluded that these should have been in existence long before the times of *Bhasa*.

From the third act of the *Pratimanataka*, some new information is gained as to the existence of a statue-house which is not described in ancient writings. The statues of departed kings are skilfully constructed in stones and erected in the statue-houses and worshipped by priests. The conclusion may therefore be drawn that it was customary to build statue-houses in the times of *Bhasa*.

34. A Rare information obtained from Pratima

Only those marked by the sterling worth of their character have been chosen to represent the heroes of these Rupakas and their movements in life both mentally and physically are so delineated as to draw the minds of the readers to follow their parts and not act otherwise.

35. The richness and perfection of the characters.

Although the hero of *Avimaraka* * is made to creep stealthily into "*Kanyapura*" at dead of night, yet even this incident is portrayed as preparatory to the bringing about of the *Gandharva* form of marriage between the lovers, and could be construed as imparting the moral that even men of heroic type and sterling character are in danger of being allured by the syren temptation of Cupid, and that one should be well guarded against such temptations.

The *Charudatta* delineating fictitious events might well be regarded as furnishing a clue to the deeds of noble and ignoble men. The other Rupakas embodying, as they are, the lives of *Sri Rama*, *Krishna*, *Yudhishthira*, *Udayana* and others are well suited to the whetting of the intellect, and as such are all of absorbing interest.

From *Bhattabana's* remarks extracted in the introduction to the *Svapnavasavadatta*, it may be inferred that the literary achievements of *Bhasa*, who is of equal rank with *Vyasa* did not extend to composing *Akhyana*, *Akhyayika* or *Mahakavya*. Whatever it might be, one thing is quite clear, that *Bhasa* considered the composing of Rupakas as the

36. Bhasa's tendency to write Rupakas.

---

* Vide appendix II. (f)

highest form of literary compositions and accordingly composed them in a remarkably exquisite form. It is quite appropriate that, of the *Kavyas*, Rupaka deserves to be placed on a higher level, as it possesses the dual characteristcs of appealing equally to both the sense of sight (दृश्य) and of hearing (श्रव्य). So this is the original form of other written compositions, as *Vamana* says in his *Kavyalankara*:—

"सन्दर्भेषु दशरूपकं श्रेयः" (1-3-30)
"दशरूपकस्यैव हीदं सर्वं विलसितं
यद्गुत कथाख्यायिके महाकाव्यमिति ।" (1-3-32)

That there was a very wide circulation of *Bhasa's* plays in *Kalidasa's* time, is evident from his own statement "प्रथितयशसां भाससौमिल्लकविपुत्रादीनां". On the other hand, its circulation had become extremely rare during the time of *Sudraka*. Thus is to be accounted for the readiness displayed by *Sudraka* in *Mrichchhakatika* to collect together the various sentences to be found in *Charudatta*; hence also the wide circulation of *Mrichchhakatika* which is merely an adaptation of another's words. These plays have thenceforward gradually disappeared from circulation and have now become extinct. How is this to be explained? Not indeed by the absence of merits, for it has already been shown that the works are so exuberant with rich ideas and are couched in such felicitous language as to attract the emulation of poets like *Kalidasa*.

87. Want of circulation of the plays of Bhasa and the absence of reference to them in the anthologies.

Nor can it be due to the omission to mention the poet's name, for *Raghuvamsa*, *Sisupalavadha* and other works wherein the author's name is not mentioned, have a wide currency.

Hence, some mysterious (अदृष्टम्) reason must be assigned for their non-circulation, on the strength of which must be explained the total disappearance, till now, except in name, of works like the *Sangraha* of *Acharya Vyadi* and the *Brihatkatha* of *Gunadhya*. It can also be explained that there s every possibility of these Rupakas becoming unused. In former times, when these Rupakas were in vogue, later poets also began to compose Rupakas. These later Rupakas, out of a personal regard to their authors, from their favourable reception at the hands of the lovers of Sanskrit, and the special encouragements at the hands of kings desirous of patronising the advancement of poetical efforts, became diffused over a large area; and gradually when further new compositions came to be produced, in large numbers, and obtained publicity, the ancient Rupakas were thrown into the background by slow degrees, and in the end vanished from the scope of literary studies. Just as in the field of Sastras, the old works, which were characterised by the excellence of their compositions, reached a decline and their very names gradually became unknown to many when later sastraic treatises, even though their merit is not of a high order, came into prominence, in the same way, the literary field being exclusively appropriated by new dramatic compositions, *Bhasa's* Rupakas came to be unknown gradually even by name. It is certain that all the Rupakas of *Bhasa*, must have been studied by *Kalidasa* and *Bhattabana*, from the fact that they praise by referring to his works in general. Of these, the *Svapnavasavadatta* and *Pratijnayaugandharayana* were, beyond doubt, in vogue at the time of the rhetorician *Vamana*; and the *Balacharita* and the *Charudatta*, in the time of *Dandin*, as is seen from their having extracted veres, as examples from them. From the fact that *Abhinavaguptacharya* mentions in his *Natyavedavivriti* the names of *Svapnavasavadatta* and *Daridra Charudatta*, it could be concluded that the said Rupakas used to be studied in his time. The other Rupakas might have been forgotten during the times of *Vamana* and others: and hence I think no verses have been quoted by them from those works. When times were so rolling, all the *Natakas* of *Bhasa* entered the abysmal cavity of oblivion, so that the compilers of *Subhashitavali* and other anthologies by their inability to obtain copies of these *Natakas* could not extract in their compilations any of the verses from them. The following verse contained in the first act of *Avimaraka* and adopted in a slightly modified form in the *Sarnghadharapad-*

dhati (Sloka 1805) appears to have been learnt by *Sarnghadhara* only by report without even once having looked into the *Avimaraka*,

> "धर्मः प्रागेव चिन्त्यः सचिवमतिगतिः प्रेक्षितव्या स्वबुद्धया
> प्रच्छाद्यौ रागशेषौ मृदुपरुषगुणौ कालयोगेन कार्यौ ।
> ज्ञेयं लोकानुवृत्तं परचरनयनैर्मण्डलं प्रेक्षितव्यं
> रक्ष्यो यत्नादिहात्मा रणशिरसि पुनः सोऽपि नावेक्षितव्यः ॥ " (sl. 12).

It is on account of this that *Sarngadhara* was not able to indicate in his work even the name of the author or of the work containing the verse. As for the few verses which are not found in the *Natakas* under discussion, but embodied in the *Subhashitavali* and other works as belonging to *Bhasa*, I think they might have been extracted from the other *Natakas* of *Bhasa* (than those in our possession) by the compilers of the anthologies. It is not certain that *Bhasa* composed only the 13 natakas now obtained, for there is nothing to indicate that he has not composed any more than these. Or it might be that the anthologists, having not actually seen the works of *Bhasa*, have ascribed these verses to *Bhasa*, believing in some tradition which so ascribed them to him. The compilers of anthologies are found to embody in their works the verses of other writers which they happened to memorise merely from their repute without having learned them from the original works themselves. * It may therefore be concluded that the *Natakas* of *Bhasa*, now under reference, had no currency in the literary activities of the times even many centuries ago. More about this later on.

38. The popularity of the plays in the Kerala country in ancient days.

There is a peculiar class of actors(कुशीलवजाति) in this country known among the people as 'Chakyar'. These people are found acting the *Nagananda* and the third act of *Pratijnayaugandharayana* which they call *Mantranka-Nataka*, on occasions of some temple festivals,

* It should be borne in mind that many of the names of the authors and works given by the anthologists are found to be incorrect.

in a method peculiar to them. It appears to me that the third act of *Pratijnayaugandharayana* is designated by them as *Mantranka*, on account of its embodying the state-craft employed by *Yaugandharayana*, the Prime Minister. But these actors are quite ignorant of the *Pratijnayaugandharayana* and the context of the *Mantranka*. Certainly at the time when *Bhasa's Natakas* were current in this country, the scholars of this country extracted this *Mantranka* from the *Pratijnanatika* and taught and laid down the method of enacting it, as in the case of the *Nagananda*. In course of time, however, when these natakas lost their publicity, the origin of the *Mantranka* itself became unknown to the very actors themselves.

39. The probability of the existence of the manuscripts of the plays of Bhasa in some corners of India.

Although these Rupakas became unknown to the world, still, I think a few of their copies may surely exist in some corners of this land of *Bharata* in the form of manuscripts, with leaves worn out by time or in fragments of manuscripts eaten off by mice and white ants. As in this State a few copies of the plays were unexpectedly brought to light so it is not unlikely that some other copies may yet be discovered in other parts of India. That such manuscripts do not exist in other parts could only be ascertained after a house-to-house search is carefully made from Kashmir to Cape Comorin.

40. Some contrary views and their refutation.

With the conclusions thus established on the basis of the materials and inferences as aforesaid, the vast majority of reasearch scholars, Indian and foreign, express their agreement; and adduce fresh arguments in fortification of the same. But it appears from the "Indian Antiquary" and some other journals that there are, here and there, a few learned men who dissent from the various conclusions. One writer says that the discovered dramas are not in fact those of *Bhasa* and another that they were composed by an unknown author who lived in the 7th century after Christ and who closely imitated *Bhasa*. Another concedes that *Bhasa* is the author of these plays but is of opinion that he lived some time in the interval between *Asvaghosha* and *Kalidasa*. A third writer holds the view that the stanza नवं शरावं सलिलैः सुपूर्णं (Act. 4) found in the *Pratijnayaugandharayana* was taken from *Kautalya's Arthasastra*. Yet another writer is of opinion that it would be impossible to establish the priority of *Bhasa* to *Panini* on the ground of the archaic forms in use in his dramas. And all these writers have advanced various arguments in support of their several views. It has now to be examined whether these arguments are capable of supporting the several conclusions based thereon.

(a) Ramavatara Sarma.

In the first part of the Allahabad Sanskrit Journal, Sarada, one Ramavatara Sarma writes:—These dramas were not written by *Bhasa* because none of the stanzas about ten in number mentioned as *Bhasa's* in *Subhashitavali* and other anthologies are to be found in them and also because none of the Nandi stanzas are dedicated to Siva as might be expected of Siva-devotee such as *Bhasa* undoubtedly was as witness the stanza,

"पेयासुरा प्रियतमामुखमीक्षितव्यं ग्राह्यः स्वभावललितो विकृतश्च वेषः ।
येनेदमीदृशमदृश्यत मोक्षवर्त्म दीर्घायुरस्तु भगवान् स पिनाकपाणिः ॥"

mentioned in his name in the anthologies. True. Though none of those stanzas are found in any of the thirteen plays we have published, it may, however, be assumed that the source of these verses might be other plays of *Bhasa* (than those already discovered), as all the plays of *Bhasa* are not yet known. But I think most probably the anthologists might have been led astray by false reports current in their times in attributing these verses to *Bhasa*. For instance, *Somaveda*, the author of *Yasastilaka*, attributed the verse "पेया सुरा प्रियतमामुखमीक्षितव्यं —" to *Bhasa* which is in fact found in the farce called *Mattavilasaprahasana* written by the Pallava King Mahendra Vikrama Varma I, son of Simhavishnu Varma who flourished early in the 7th cent. A. D. The verse as it occurs in that work is from a Kapalika and only describes the religious tenets of the Kapalika sect which were condemned by the followers of all other creeds. It is therefore curious to observe that this verse, which the author of *Yasastilaka* ascribed by mistake to *Bhasa*, should have led Ramavatara Sarma to hazard inferences about *Bhasa* that he was a devotee of Siva and the like.

Another writer, Bhattanathaswami, writes thus in the Journal of the Indian Antiquary (P. 189. Vol. XLV, 1916) "The *Svapnavasavadatta* mentioned by *Sarvananda* in his commentary *Amaratikasarvasva*, must be different from the drama of the same name, published in the Trivandrum Sanskrit series, because in commenting on the stanza " शृङ्गारवीरक-रुणा – the author says " Sringara is divisible into three classes viz.' धर्म, अर्थ and काम. The first is instanced in *Nandayanti* where the Brahmin is feasted; the second, in the marriage of *Padmavati* by *Udayana* with the object of recovering back his territories and the same man's marriage of *Vasavadatta* in *Svapnavasavadatta* is an illustration of कामशृङ्गार; and from this it is clear that the main theme of *Svapnavasavadatta* was the marriage of *Vasavadatta* and not of *Padmavati*, whereas in the published *Svapnavasavadatta* the story relates to a period subsequent to the marriage of *Vasavadatta* and deals with that of *Padmavati*.

(b) Bhattanatha Swami.

2. "And the stanza "स्वश्रितपक्ष्मकवाटं–" expressly mentioned in ध्वन्यालोकलोचन as taken from *Svapnavasavadatta* and not found in the published drama must have been taken from the other drama of the same name as mentioned above.

3. "The story of that other *Svapnavasavadatta* must have been this, viz., that *Vasavadatta*, having once seen *Udayana* in a dream, fell in love with him and informing him of the same, married him, though she had been promised by her father to *Sanjaya*, because here the stanza "स्वश्रितपक्ष्मकवाटं—" could well have been used to describe the first springs of love of the hero towards *Vasavadatta* and also there will be special appropriateness in the name of the drama of which the main theme is the dream which *Vasavadatta* has of *Udayana* and which results in their marriage. Neither is it proper to cast

any doubt on the genuineness of the story on the ground that it does not find a place in the *Kathasaritsagara*; because its existence is attested by Prof. Wilson who mentions it on the authority of the commentators of *Meghasandesa* in connection with the stanza "प्राप्यावन्तीनुदयनकथाकोविदग्रामवृद्धान्—" (पूर्व० श्लो. 30).

4. "And this story is further alluded to in *Malati-Madhava* Act II, where *Kamandaki* says 'and *Vasavadatta* married *Udayana* while her father had promised her to king *Sanjaya*'. And this passage establishes not only the existence of the story but also of the very drama having this story for its plot. For in the opening lines of the speech of *Kamandaki*, just quoted viz. '*Sakuntala*, daughter of *Visvamitra*, loved *Dushyanta* and the nymph *Urvasi*, *Pururavas*', the reference to the stories of *Sakuntala* and *Urvasi* is clearly to the dramas of *Sakuntala* and *Vikramorvasiya* as suggested by Dr. Bhandarkar in his edition of *Malati-Madhava*. It stands to reason that the passage dealing with *Vasavadatta* standing as it does with two others referring to dramas, should be construed as likewise referring to a drama, describing the marriage of *Vasavadatta*.

5. "And that drama thus shown to have dealt with the story of *Vasavadatta* must have been *Bhasa's Svapnavasavadatta* as it is referred to by a master-poet like *Bhavabhuti*.

"Thus the *Svapnavasavadatta* published in the Trivandrum Sanskrit Series is shown to be materially different from the true and ancient *Svapnavasavadatta*, and besides, it does not agree with the drama mentioned by *Sarvananda* and the author of *Lochana*; and therefore it is the work not of *Bhasa*, but of a later poet to whom must be ascribed also the authorship of the connected plays, *Charudatta* and others."

"It will thus be seen that the statement that the *Mrichchhakatika* is based on *Charudatta* is wholly untenable because it rests on the theory that *Charudatta* was the work of the ancient poet *Bhasa*, which is shown to be wrong. On the other hand, it is now patently clear that *Charudatta* is based on *Mrichchhakatika*".

All this is on its very face unprepossessing and illogical, A thing whose existence is possible can be established, even though invisible, by process of reasoning, but not a thing whose existence is impossible. Now once when a drama called *Svapnavasavadatta* is shown to be actually in existence, how is it possible to establish the existence of a second *Svapnavasavadatta?* In the face of the well-known drama called *Svapnavasavadatta* written by an ancient and a great dramatist and admired by generations of literary critics, will any writer attempt to palm off a drama of his own under the same name? It will be a most futile task. If the story and plot be identical, even then with a view to avoid confusion as to identity, different names ought to be given to the drama such as *Mahaviracharita*, *Anargharaghava*, etc. In case the story and plot be different, the name should be selected so as to bring out that very difference as in *Uttararamacharita* etc. But then it might be said that a writer naming his own composition after the work of another writer might be moved by considerations of his own benefit or distinction with a view to produce a compendious version of that other work. If so, let us examine how it can be. It might be that the later writer might think, "Here is a story dramatized by an ancient poet, I will also dramatize the same story, and furthermore I will name it after the very drama of the ancient poet, so that the critics might easily compare the merit of the two works and pronounce the superior excellence of my composition and honor me accordingly." That might be alleged a motive. But it cannot be. For *ex hypothesi* the story and plot of the drama are distinct, because as mentioned above the main theme of the imaginary *Svapnavasavadatta* is stated to be the dream by *Vasavadatta* of *Udayana*, her love for him, and their marriage, whereas in the published drama the main story is subsequent to the marriage of *Vasavadatta*. And in case subject matters are different it is impossible to challenge a comparison on the merits of the two dramas, as for instance, the *Mahaviracharita* and *Uttararamacharita* which deal with two different stories. As for the suggestion that the later writer might have been moved by considerations of his own benefit or distinction, that is extremely unlikely, because it would otherwise be inexplicable why he should not have mentioned his name therein even departing from the practice of his age. For the same reason, it is clear that the object of the later writer could not have been to produce a compendium of the earlier work, because the subjects and plots of the two dramas are different. But it could be argued that the name of the older drama does not correctly describe the subject matter therein and that the later drama of the same name correctly describes the subject matter therein and was written with a view to bring the above discrepancy to the notice of the critics. If it is so argued, this is inconsistent with the argument for the other side that the present drama is not properly named with reference to its contents, whereas the other drama must have been properly named. Then it might be said that a later and a modern writer might have written this drama under the name of *Svapnavasavadatta* and suppressed his name therein thinking "at some future time when *Bhasa's* *Svapnavasavadatta* passes out of circulation, then by some lucky accident, some critic will get hold of this *Svapnavasavadatta* of mine and mistaking this for *Bhasa's* work confer upon me, an unknown man, all the honors of the mistake and then my labours shall be rewarded." If such a motive be ever attributed to the author of this drama, we have to impute the greatest meanness to him. And to attribute such a meanness would in itself be a meanness. Thus we might start with the conclusion that there could not have been two dramas with the name of *Svapnavasavadatta.*

The above argument answers the argument based on the passage quoted from the *Amarakosatikasarvasva* as to the existence of the second *Svapnavasavadatta* having for its plot the story of *Vasavadatta's* marriage. And when once the conclusion is reached that this drama could have been the only drama of the name of *Svapnavasavadatta*, the passage in the *Amarakosatikasarvasva* can well be construed as applying to our drama and not to an imaginary one, shown to have been never in existence. The passage from the *Tikasarvasva* has already been extracted in full (*supra*). In that passage after mentioning the kinds of Sringara, Dharma, Artha and Kama, the drama *Nandayanti* is given as instance of the first and the *Svapnavasavadatta* is mentioned as illustration of both the others. And the words in the *Svapnavasavadatta* must be read along with the second as well as the third clauses. Thus the meaning of the passage is that in the *Svapnavasavadatta* the marrying of *Padmavati* is described as prompted by the motive of winning back a kingdom and is therefore a case of Artha-Sringara, while the marrying of *Vasavadatta* already accomplished was prompted by mere love for love's sake and is the case of Kama Sringara. If, in the passage, we take the reference to *Svapnavasavadatta* as applying to Kama Sringara alone, we should then say that the author of the *Tikasarvasva* having given the reference in the first and the third cases has omitted it in the second case which amounts to making him faulty of giving defective information and of dissimilar treatment of similar subjects. And the plot of our *Svapnavasavadatta* which bears the distinctive marks noticed, shows unmistakably that both the Artha and Kama Sringaras are referred to by him. This meaning of his, which of course is the meaning of the passage, will, we think, be made still clearer if the order of the words तृतीय and स्वप्नवासवदत्ते in the passage be exchanged.

And when it is thus shown that the very theory of a second drama of the name of *Svapnavasavadatta* is nothing but a castle in the air, why should we further consider the argument that the stanza "स्वञ्चितपक्ष्मकवाटं नयनद्वारं" quoted in the *Lochana* should be taken to have been quoted from it ? Who then is *Bhasa* ? What are the special characteristics of his *Svapnavasavadatta* by which we can identify the present drama with *Bhasa's* ? We proceed to answer. Let us consider these utterances of *Kalidasa, Bhatta—Bana Rajasekhara* and *Ramachandra*, "प्रथितयशसां भाससौमिल्लकविपुत्रादीनां (*Malavikagnimitra*, Act I), "सूत्रधारकृतारम्भैर्नाटकै–" (*Harshacharita*), "भासनाटकचक्रेऽपि–" (*Suktimuktavali*), यथाभासकृते स्वप्नवासवदत्ते (*Natyadarpana*). From the above passages we learn that there was a very ancient poet by the name of *Bhasa*, that he was the author of many *Natakas* ond that *Svapnavasavadatta* was one of them. It follows therefore that *Svapnavasavadatta* must be distinctly marked by a close resemblance to certain other *Natakas* many in number, by qualities of diction and expression indicative of priority to the works of *Kalidasa* add thirdly by a plot appropriate to the name of *Svapnavasavadatta.*

Now let us examine whether these three distinguishing marks are found in our *Nataka* which has the name of *Svapnavasavadatta* written at the end. With regard to the first of these characteristics, even a cursory reading of the thirteen natakas that have come into our ken cannot fail to convince one of their very close resmblance and this point has already been dealt on at some length in the introductions to the *Svapnavasavadatta* and *Pancharatra*. That our *Nataka* possesses the second characteristic mark also is indicated in these introductions and also in the introduction to the *Pratimanataka*. This is obvious to those whose sense of the beautiful has been refined by the words and the images of the great sages like *Valmiki* and *Vyasa* and who can perceive the shades of aesthetic difference in the sweet words and beautiful ideas of different poets. Who that is blessed with an aesthetic sense, who that tastes that unique natural flow of beauty that overflows the sound and sense of every passage and particularly of every short piece of prose in these natakas, can for a moment doubt their priority to the works of *Kalidasa?* Again the verse, नवं शरावं सलिलैः सुपूर्णं सुसंस्कृतं, quoted as from another's work by *Kautalya* in his *Arthasastra* is in its proper place in the *Pratijnayaugandharayana* and can from its very nature be seen to be the poet's own. It is because it is appropriate only to Kavya that *Vamana* who lived decidedly before *Anandavardhana*, the author of Dhvani, (in the chapter of his *Kavyalankara* devoted to the criticism of expressions used in Kavyas and Kavyas alone) takes up for consideration the fourth quarter of the verse 'यो भर्तृपिण्डस्य कृते न युध्येत्' and attempts to justify the use of Parasmaipada therein. Hence *Vamana* must have known for certain that this verse belonged to a Kavya. Otherwise he would not have taken it for consideration right in the midst of expressions culled from Kavyas alone. It follows that *Pratijnayaugandharayana* from which *Chanakya* quotes the verse and the other *Natakas* that are akin to it including of course *Svapnavasavadatta* belong to a period much earlier than that of *Chanakya* and therefore earlier still than that of *Kalidasa* who is known to have lived long after *Chanakya*.

Considering the third distinguishing mark which our natakas must be shown to bear before it could be identified with *Bhasa's Svapnavasavadatta*, we have to look to the significance of the name "*Svapnavasavadatta*". It means that in this work *Vasavadatta* is seen or attended to (by *Vatsaraja*) in his dream. This is just what we learn from the conversation in the fifth act of our nataka where *Vatsaraja* brooding on the supposed loss of his *Vasavadatta* and beside himself with grief, talks to her in his dream, and she, in all reality awake by his side though not known to him, listens to and responds to his lamenting words. Here in this dream, *Vasavadatta* fully perceived the great depth and intense sincerity of his ardent love and this knowledge nourishes and developes the prominent Rasa in her, i. e., the sentiment of separation from her love by blowing her constant fire of love to burn with a greater blaze. It is in this dream that *Vatsaraja* enjoyed to his confounding surprise the sight and touch of living *Vasavadatta*, who, he believed, was all lost to him. Having considered the importance of the Svapna or dream, we will now view the part played by *Vasavadatta*. She is at once seen to be the chief heroine courting adversity in the interests of her husband and, undaunted by the troubles that beset her and ever skilfully vigilant to the purpose before her, she, the type of perfect womanhood, shines on high in the varied glory of her beauty, virtue, wisdom, fortitude and nobility. *Padmavati*, on the other hand, plays but a subordinate part, the incidents associated with her being brought in only to brighten up the picture of the chief heroine. Thus we see that the name *Svapnavasavadatta* is most appropriate to a work wherein the incident of the Svapna and the character, *Vasavadatta*, are seen to be so important.

As we have seen that our nataka possesses the three characteristic marks which determine *Bhasa's Svapnavasavadatta*, it can indisputably be identified with that work. Hence with the help of this *Nataka* of ours which is *Bhasa's Svapnavasavadatta* itself, we can test whether a particular verse or idea, considered in any other work as taken from *Svapnavasavadatta*, is actually so or not; and if any verse said to be taken from *Svapnavasavadatta* is found worthy of a place in our nataka, but not actually read in it, then it has to be considered as an omission in our manuscripts owing to the plays having ceased from circulation for a long time. In the wide world of our Rhetoric literature there is but one verse, "स्वाञ्चितपक्ष्मकवाटं नयनद्वारं स्वरूप(तड ?) ताडेन।" considered as taken from *Svapnavasavadatta* and this verse occurs only in *Dhvanyalokalochana*. The verse neither finds nor can it find a place in the *Svapnavasavadatta* we have procured. Hence we conclude that the author of the *Lochana* must have erroneously assigned the verse to *Svapnavasavadatta*. A similar mistake is made by *Somadeva* in his *Yasastilaka* when he assigns to *Bhasa* the verse "पेया सुरा प्रियतमामुखमीक्षितव्यं" which ought to have been correctly assigned to Mahendra Vikrama Varman I.

Now coming to the imaginary *Svapnavasavadatta* drama and to the appropriateness of the name to the story as fancied by Bhattanathaswami, that is likewise unsound. For, the case for the other side is that the story rests on the vision of *Udayana* by *Vasavadatta* in dream, the love kindled by such vision and their eventual marriage. And so far as the name of the drama gives prominence to the dream, that is correct; but when it comes to giving a preference between the person who dreams and the person who is dreamt of, it should undoubtedly have been in favour of *Udayana* who is the object seen in vision and the object to be obtained by the result of such vision; and the drama should have been more properly called '*Svapnodayana*' and not '*Svapnavasavadatta*'. As for the three-fold inappropriateness in the dream in the present drama, namely, (1) the dream being based on the love of *Udayana* for *Vasavadatta* which in his own words "had become as it were blunt", (2) the very unreal nature of the dream, and (3) the accidental absence of *Padmavati* from *Samudragriha* where her bedding had been arranged, it is also a misapprehension. Because, even things long forgotten might suddenly be revealed to us in dreams and because the pangs of *Udayana* for *Vasavadatta* which are shown to have been keen throughout the drama are only shown, in the passage above said by the words 'blunt' and 'as it were', to have come within the limits of endurance; and besides they had been further edged on the eve of the dream "स्मराम्यवन्त्याधिपतेः सुतायाः प्रस्थानकाले स्वजनं स्मरन्त्याः । बाष्पं प्रवृद्धं नयनान्तलग्नं स्नेहान्ममैवोरसि पातयन्त्याः ।" (स्वप्न अ. 5). Thus the dream being in accordance with the general notion that it reproduces our thoughts while awake, is specially appropriate. The absence of *Padmavati* from the *Samudragriha* where her bedding had been arranged is easily explained by supposing her to have been too weary and too ill to move to *Samudragriha* or by supposing her to have gently slept where she had been lying before; and the reason why the poet has not expressly mentioned it might have been that he presumed on the imagination of the readers. The story of *Svapnavasavadatta* as sketched by Bhattanathaswami must also be rejected for the reason that it is not borne out anywhere and rests purely on his own imagination. As for the statement of Professor Wilson that the story was so told by commentators of *Meghasandesa* in connection with the stanza "प्राप्यावन्तीनुदयकथाकोविदग्रामवृद्धान्" how can it be accepted in the absence of the authorities from which the stories should have been taken? For this is not mentioned by *Dakshinavarta*, *Purnasarasvati*, *Mallinatha* and others in their commentaries. Then coming to the passage in the *Malati Madhava*, Act II, wherein *Kamandaki* informs *Malati* that *Vasavadatta* married *Udayana* who was her own choice in defiance of her father's wishes, it must be noted that the context of the passage is that *Kamandaki* wants to encourage *Malati* in preferring a lover of her own choice and on that occasion this story of *Vasavadatta* as also that of *Sakuntala* and *Urvasi* is touched. But there is nothing to show that the story so touched is cast in the mould which Bhattanathaswami conceives; for there is nothing about the dream in the passage. Therefore it is clear that the argument of the other side that the said passage is a veiled allusion to the supposed drama of *Svapnavasavadatta* with the dream by *Vasavadatta* and the marriage of *Udayana* is thoroughly untenable. And further though it may be right to say that *Bhavabhuti* had in mind some ancient works while writing the passage of *Kamandaki* referring to *Sakuntala* etc., is it not better to suppose that he was thinking of that store-house of all stories, *Mahabharata*, rather than works like *Sakuntala* based thereon? It is further contended by the other side that the quotati n by *Vamana* in his *Kavyalankara* "यासां बलिर्भवति......" which is found both in *Mrichchhakatika* and *Charudatta* must be taken to prove only the acquaintance with *Mrichchhakatika* and not *Charudatta* because the auther quotes also the passage, "द्यूतं हि नाम पुरुषस्यासिंहासनं राज्यम्" which is found in *Mrichchhakatika* but not in *Charudatta* and also because *Sudraka* is praised in another passage for making a free use of the Slesha (the Guna) in his works with which *Vamana* must necessarily have been acquainted. But this is not so, because *Vamana*'s knowledge of both *Svapnavasavadatta* and *Pratijnayaugandharayana* is proved by his quoting "शरच्छशाङ्कगौरेण etc.," which is found in *Svapnavasavadatta* (Act 1) and "यो भर्तृपिण्डस्य कृते न युध्येत्" which is a part of the stanza "नवं शरावं" (Act 4) found in

Pratijnayaugandharayana; and therefore it follows that he should have known the sister drama *Charudatta*. And it is not to be argued that because *Vamana* knew *Mrichchhakatika* therefore he could not have known *Charudatta*. Why shoul he not have known both? Then coming to the mention of *Sudraka* by *Vamana* in connection with Slesha; by Slesha is meant the intricate and subtle evolution of the story and the plot and when *Sudraka* is praised for this quality, it clearly means that he has improved *Charudatta* into *Mrichchhakatika* by new and intricate plots. It must also be understood that it is not expressly mentioned that *Bhasa* is so rich in Slesha as *Sudraka* because *Mrichchhakatika* is based on *Charudatta*.

And this dreamer who imagines a second drama of the name of *Svapnavasavadatta* after having set out at full length the arguments aforesaid finally sums up thus: "The Svapna-vasavadatta which is now before us is too modern to be Bhasa's composition". Now the present drama can be said to be modern either because it is shown to have been written by a modern author or because its merits as a composition, its style and matter might be said to negative its claim to be old. But the former is not the case as it is not shown who the modern author of this drama is. And the latter cannot be the case as no argument has been advanced against its antiquity on any investigation of its matter and style. On the other hand, if we consider the merits of the compositions, their antiquity is clear beyond any shadow of doubt, as in fact they are even superior, as shown in our commentaries on *Svapnavasavadatta* and others, to *Kalidasa's* works. It is unnecessary to further consider the wholly misguided and futile arguments of Bhattanathaswami.

(c) Dr. L. D. Barnett.

The theory of Dr. Barnett that the author of the dramas could not have been *Bhasa* but a writer who lived in the seventh century A. D. stands disproved by the foregoing discussion. It cannot be that the works which are shown to have been anterior to *Kalidasa* could well be placed in the 7th century A. D. The arguments advanced by Dr. Barnett in support of the above theory are untenable. They are two in number. One is the close similarity between the present plays and *Mattavilasaprahasana*, a farce written in the seventh century A. D. and the other is the reference to the king *Rajasimha* which is found in the *Bharatavakya* stanzas and it is said that *Rajasimha* lived in the 7th century A. D. As for the alleged similarity, it is not so. Because, it can be either similarity in the form of the composition or in its substance. It cannot be the former because our dramas differ from the farce even in form. In our dramas there is no mention of the name of either the poet or his work which is found in *Mattavilasa*; and inasmuch as the practice of mentioning the name of the poet and his work which had been in vogue from the time of *Kalidasa* and during the 7th century, is not adopted by our poet, that itself is the strongest evidence in favour of the antiquity of our dramas and the strongest argument against the theory of their having been composed in the 7th century A. D. Coming to the substance of *Mattavilasa*, it will be found that, whereas these dramas excel in point of diction and sentiment even *Kalidasa's* works, and are on a par with the works of *Valmiki* and *Vyasa*, the *Mattavilasaprahasana* is clearly modern in point of style as well as poetic merits. And there is also the fact that in the *Mattavilasa*, there is no archaism such as is found in *Bhasa's* plays. The second argument of Dr. Barnett in favour of the 7th century is answered thus. When once it is established by independent reasoning that *Bhasa* should have lived long anterior to the 7th century, it cannot be that he could refer to a king of the name of *Rajasimha* in the seventh century. But in fact the word *Rajasimha* is not at all a proper name referring to any particular king. For one thing it would be highly improper for any subject to speak of his king barely by his name like his father or mother. And also the *Bharatavakyas* in some of the dramas viz, "राजा भूमिं प्रशास्तु नः" (in *Pratima*) "गां पातु नो नरपतिः" (in *Urubhanga*) "राजा राजगुणोपेतो भूमिमेकः प्रशास्तु नः" (in *Karnabhara*), only speak of one's own king in general and it would be proper only to construe '*Rajasimha*' as meaning a great king; and this construction has the merit of giving consistency and uniformity in all the *Bharataaakyas*. Besides, the word *Rajasimha* is frequently met with in the sense of "the best of kings" in the Sundara-Kanda and Balakanda of the *Ramayana*; and as *Bhasa* is a follower of the *Ramayana*, it is proper to take that he used the word in the sense that we give it. We accordingly find him using the expression "Nripatisimha" in the sense of *Rajasimha* in "मुदितनृपतिसिंह" (*Karnabhara*).

It is gratifying to note that Dr. F. W. Thomas of the India Office, London, has also dealt with the inconsistencies of the theory of Dr. L. D. Barnett (Vide pp. 79-83, Journal of R. A. S. of Great Britain and Ireland, January 1922.)

As for our observation in the introduction to the *Svapnavasavadatta* that "सूत्रधारकृतारम्भैरिति भट्टबाणोक्तं सूत्रधारकृतारम्भत्वं भासकृतीनामसाधारणो धर्मः कामं प्रत्येतुं शक्यः", it was not advanced by us as our main argument for establishing the authorship of *Bhasa*, but having estabtished it by other and conclusive arguments, we added that our dramas answered also to the description of *Bana*, and this circumstance might be regarded as a piece of evidence in our favour. That being so, we are bound to add that we are not in entire agreement with * Mr. Banerjee Sastri who appears to lay undue emphasis on the fact that the dramas open with the entry of *Sutradhara*. Though, as *Bana* says, *Bhasa* might have been responsible for this, as nevertheless, it has been followed in other later plays like *Subhadradhananjaya*, it cannot be said that this arrangement excludes the ownership of the plays of any other author except *Bhasa*.

As regards our observation that these dramas abound in that natural beauty which is itself an indication of their ancient origin and the like and which is to be found only in the writings of *Valmiki* and *Vyasa*, no one has taken objection to it. But some are of opinion that the Prakrit forms found in these dramas are akin to those used by *Kalidasa* and therefore suggest a more modern age. In his treatise on

* Vide PP 367—382, J. R. A. S. of Great Britain and Ireland, July 1921.

" The Prakrit of *Bhasa* " Dr. Printz expresses the view that the Prakrit is ancient; while Dr. Lenzy is of opinion that it is more modern than *Asvaghosha's*. Mahamahopadhyaya Haraprasada Sastri and others think that the Prakrit, though it might have been ancient, as written by the poet, might nevertheless have been modernized by the copyists of a later age and the original Prakrit forms might have thus undergone a change. And it is because of this uncertainty as to the real original Prakrit forms that Dr. Barnett says that they could not be strongly depended upon in determining the age (P. 587 Journal of R. A. S. October 1921).

Now coming to the first of the various views aforesaid viz. the close similarity between the Prakrit of *Bhasa* and *Kalidasa* it has been shown in page 58 *supra* that this could be possible even though centuries might have elapsed between the two writers. The second and the fourth views mentioned above are in favour of the view we have taken. Likewise the last-mentioned view. For, Dr. Barnett, being of opinion that the dramas were composed in the seventh century A. D. had to meet arguments against his view based on the antiquity of the Prakrit forms and has shown that too much reliance could not be placed on them. This argument is equally available to negative the views of Dr. Lenzy and Mr. Banerjee Sastri that *Bhasa* must have been later than *Asvaghosha* and earlier than *Kalidasa* because they rest on an examination of the Prakrit. But when we say that the Prakrit is not material we speak with exclusive reference to the forms in Prakrit and not their Sanskrit equivalents; because the latter are as simple and sweet as the original Sanskrit sentences of the author, and along with latter, enable us to determine their age, and thus become material. Thus the third of the views aforesaid also stands answered. This view is also open to this further criticism, that their authors do not even controvert our view stated in the introduction to *Pratimanataka* that *Asvaghosha* has very largely drawn from *Bhasa*, much less show that *Bhasa* was indebted to *Asvaghosha*, as they ought to have shown.

(d) Messrs. Krishna Pisharodi and Rama Pisharodi.

In the Bulletin of the School of Oriental Studies, London, at PP. 107-117 of III. 1, are to be found some criticisms by Messrs. Krishna Pisharodi and Rama Pisharodi on my views of *Bhasa* and his authorship of *Svapnavasavadatta* and the connected dramas published in the Trivandrum Sanskrit Series. Their arguments are summarised hereunder with replies thereto.

I. "Every open-minded critic must preforce admit that *Pratimanataka* must come after *Kalidasa*, *Charudatta* after *Sudraka* and *Avimaraka* after *Dandin*.

(1) ' As regards *Pratima*, the geneology of *Raghu's* dynasty as described therein agrees with that in the *Raghuvamsa*. And therefore *Pratima* is based on *Raghuvamsa*. And it must be taken that that geneology was the creation of *Kalidasa* because *Valmiki* makes no mention of it. In *Pratima* the geneology is referred to only in passing. It is legitimate to infer from this that it had been well established, having been already described in detail elsewhere; and it is so described in *Kalidasa*. So say the Pishardis.

But it was not open to *Kalidasa* any more than to *Bhasa* to manufacture a new geneology. It must necessarily be inferred that some *Itihasa* other than *Ramayana* must have served as the basis for them both. Accordingly both *Dakshinavartanatha* and *Arunachalanatha* after stating that the geneology in *Raghuvamsa* follows that in *Vishnupurana*, quote the following passage from *Vishnupurana* in commenting on 3rd Sarga, 21st stanza.

" मूलकाद् दशरथः, तस्माद् दिलिपः, ततश्च विश्वसहः, तस्माच्च खट्वाङ्गो दिलीपः, खट्वाङ्गाद् रघुरभवद्, रघोरजः, अजाद् दशरथः ।"

(*Vishnupurana*, Amsa 4, Adhyaya 4) *

It was only after establishing by other reasons that *Bhasa* must have been the author of *Pratima* that we stated in our

---

* "First Mulaka, then Dasaratha, then Dilipa, then Visvasaha, then Khatvanga Dilipa, from Khatvanga Raghu, from Raghu Aja, from Aja Dasaratha."

introduction to it that *Kalidasa* followed *Bhasa* even in the geneology. It was not sought by us to establish the priority of *Pratima* to *Kalidasa* by reason of the idendity of the geneology in the writers. And as the authority for the geneology is to be found in another *Itihasa*, its identity in *Pratima* and *Raghuvamsa* is incapable of establishing the priority of either in relation to the other. Therefore all discussions based upon the fullness of the description or otherwise of the geneology are all futile.

2. With reference to *Charudatta* the argument of the Pisharodis is that it is an abridgement of *Mrichchhakatika*; that the story forming the subject matter of the six Acts, Acts V to X, was omitted for the convenience of the actors in Kerala and, to save time, that an easy diction was adopted so that it might be easily understood and that *Charudatta* is a complete drama in itself.

But it is not so; because before establishing the priority of *Mrichchhakatika* to *Charudatta* and the connected dramas of *Svapnavasavadatta* and the rest, it is impossible to say that *Mrichchhakatika* is the original of *Charudatta* and that the latter is an adaptation of the former. For no reason has been adduced by the other side to establish the priority of *Mrichchhakatika*. We have, on the other hand, established the priority of *Charudatta* by showing that it must have been composed by the author of *Svapnavasavadatta*, and by other reasons; and they ought to have been met by the other side, but they have not been. Further the story related in Acts V to X of the *Mrichchhakatika* has not been omitted but retained in *Charudatta*. For *Sakara* is described in the latter as vindictive and capable of doing harm to anyone who might do him harm; and his anger is shown to have been roused by *Vasantasena* whom he loves having taken refuge in *Charudatta's* house. And *Charudatta* is described as of noble qualities. And in the fourth act *Vasantasena* sets about to meet her lover *Charudatta* in his house—which must have greately put out *Sakara*. The story thus related does certainly contemplate the fifth and the later acts. For the reader will like to know what the several trials and troubles were to which *Charudatta* must inevitably have been put by reason of the anger of *Sakara* and how in keeping with his character he was saved therefrom; and the incidents described in the later acts have to be tacked on in order to satisfy the reader's mind; and the drama must therefore be incomplete without them. The easy diction admitted on the other side is a point in favour of the priority of *Charudatta* to *Mrichchhakatika*. As for the omission of the Mangla sloka, to attribute it to "the hurry of the adapation" is highly inconsistent with the statement that the compiler of *Charudatta* is a "clever playwright."

3. Then coming to *Avimaraka*, its story is modelled on the stories of *Dasakumaracharita*; and when the Madras Government publishes the poem called *Avantisundari* it is probable that we may find many verses common to it and *Avimaraka*. Therefore *Avimaraka* is merely a compilation. So say the Pisharodis.

This reasoning is surprising. Because the stories resemble each other, it does not follow that one work is compiled from the other. Otherwise one might say that *Mahaviracharita* and other dramas dealing with the story of *Rama* must have been compilations based on one another, because the story is the same. Even if there be some verses in *Avantisundari* in common with *Avimaraka* it might be that the former adopted them from the latter, because *Avimaraka* is proved to be prior. Moreover even one such stanza has not been quoted by the other side, not even for illustration; from which it has to be gathered that the statement about the existence of many common verses rests not on the direct observation of the writers but on hearsay information implicitly adopted by them.

Thus we have negatived the main contentions of the other side, on which it was sought to make out that *Pratima*, *Charudatta*, and *Avimaraka* were later than *Kalidasa*, *Sudraka* and *Dandin*.

II. Then it is stated by the Pisharodis that the reference to the worship of statues in the third act of *Pratima* indicates that *Bhasa*, the predecessor of *Kalidasa* could not be the author of this group of dramas because in the Siva Temple at Tiruvanchikulam, the ancient capital of the Chera Kings there is a statue dedicated to Bhaskara Ravi Varman, the last of the Chera kings, and it is worshipped. In view of the connexion of this prince and of the *Svapna* group of dramas with the Kerala stage, it is proper to infer that the incident in the *Pratima* is based on this deification.

This is erroneous. The sort of *Pratima-Griha* which is described in the drama is one which is mainly intended for the installation and worship of the statues of the departed kings and not a temple dedicated to Vishnu or Siva or other deity with a statue therein of a devotee-king, the statue being put there as in the case of other devotees in honor of the king by his admirers. Bhaskara Ravi Varman was a pious man and the last of the Chera kings and, therefore, to perpetuate his memory, his admirers had his statue installed in the temple at Tiruvanchikulam. Similar statues of kings are also found in the temples in the Pandya and Chola countries. But the sort of *Pratimagriha* described in the *Pratima* is to be found nowhere. Therefore the *Pratima* incident in the drama has no connexion with the installation of the statue of Bhaskara Ravi Varman, as the installation of royal statues obtains in other countries as well as Kerala; and as the sort of *Pratimagriha* described has not the slightest trace of existence in Kerala. As for the special connection between the Kerala actors and the *Svapna* group of dramas, that connection existed with reference to other dramas as well. The Chakyar actors of Kerala acted *Nagananda*, *Mattavilasa* and other dramas as well as the *Svapna* group of dramas. This has been mentioned by us in page 79 *supra* under the heading "The popularity of the plays in Kerala country" in ancient days. And it is not logical to attribute a Kerala origin to the *Svapna* group of dramas because they were acted by Kerala actors. Otherwise we will have to attribute a Kerala origin to

Nagananda, *Mattavilasa* and the rest as they were also acted by Kerala actors.

III. In *Pratima* Act I, *Sita* is described as not participating in the coronation ceremonies of *Rama*. The practice in Kerala is that in the coronation the king sits alone without his consort. It has therefore to be inferred that *Pratima* was composed in Kerala. So argue the Pisharodis.

This argument is faulty. The coronation of *Rama* was only as a *Yuvaraja* and is of secondary importance. Moreover, *Vasishtha*, *Vamadeva* and others knew beforehand that the coronation was not going to take place * but nevertheless started it in compliance with the wishes of king *Dasaratha* and the ceremony was a mere farce. Thus there was nothing to be gained by making *Sita* participate in the ceremonies. On the other hand, the great poet has vastly gained in not making her participate. For it was by adopting this plan of separating *Sita* from *Rama* that it was possible to describe how at the very time of the coronation *Sita* became accidentally interested in wearing the *valkalam* and how she actually wore it thereby foreshadowing the forest life which was going to be. Thus suitably to her character of a chaste woman, *Sita* was able to go along with *Rama* without any delay with the very *valkalam*, when, after relinquishing the kingdom in the observance of his father's words, he was about to leave for the forests. By this plan it was also possible to arrange to present the *valkalam* to *Rama* for wearing in the forest. It would have been quite impossible to weave all these flashy incidents into the drama, had *Sita* been by the side of *Rama* at the time of the coronation. That is why the intelligent poet with a view to enhance the effect separated *Sita* from *Rama* at the time of the coronation. On the occasion of the main coronation of *Rama* as king, *Sita* is mentioned as having been with him. In the seventh act the words are "then enters *Rama* with *Sita* after coronation." § Even if we adopt the reading "then enters *Rama* with his *Parivara* after coronation" *Sita*

* See Pratima, p. 120, 1924 edition with commentary.

§ "ततः प्रविशति कृताभिषेको रामः सह सीतया ।"

must also be taken to be included in the word "*Parivara*" Likewise in the drama *Abhisheka*, on the occasion of the main coronation, the words used are "Then enters *Rama* with *Sita* after Coronation." So *Sita* is described as having been with *Rama*. Thus the surmise of the Pisharodis that some Kerala poet must have introduced the practice of his country in describing the hero's story is without any foundation whatever. It certainly does appear to me to be surprising that the surmise aforesaid leads to this that the poet who so erroneously adopts his local practice in describing a different hero must be deemed to be very careless or worse.

IV. Then the Pisharodis say "The antiquity of the Sanskrit and Prakrit adduced to justify and support the *Bhasa* theory is in reality only an ingenious myth."

This also is wrong. It is not shown that it is only an ingenious myth. Every person who is well acquainted with the ancient and the later Sanskrit works will unhesitatingly accept the antiquity of the Sanskrit in *Bhasa*. In fact, in our introduction to *Pratima* we have shown that it is more ancient than not merely *Kalidasa* but also *Asvaghosha*; and all that has not been challenged. The Pisharodis are silent on this but merely state it as their *ipse dixit* that there is not that natural beauty which would prove the antiquity of this group of dramas and they do not advance anything to establish this statement. But a mere statement is not proof of the matters stated. As for the statement that "the general tone of simplicity is easily explained when it is remembered that these dramas were produced not with a literary purpose nor to glorify a king or national event, but mainly as we shall show later with a view to meet the demands of a flourishing popular stage," we ask whether the adoption of a simple diction does or does not militate against the merits of the dramas as literary compositions. If it does militate, then it must be admitted that the easy diction in dramas like *Sakuntala* is out of place. If it does not, then the same considerations apply both to dramas like *Sakuntala* and the present ones. As a matter of fact, the view of the critics is that the literary merits of a composition rise in proportion to the simplicity of the diction. That the diction in these dramas is even simpler than in *Sakuntala* only shows that their author excels even *Kalidasa*. We will deal later on with this meeting "the demands of a flourishing popular stage". Though the Prakrit in these dramas is similar to that of *Kalidasa*, that is not a point against their antiquity as shown by us in page 53 *supra*. After establishing by independent reasons that *Bhasa* must have been the author of these dramas we stated that their Prakrit was in keeping with their antiquity. If our conclusion is to be challenged our reasons therefor ought first to be met; and they are not met merely by stating that there is similarity between the Prakrit of these dramas and the Prakrit in *Sakuntala*, *Subhadradhananjaya* and other later dramas. When the Prakrit of the ancient dramas came conventionally to be adopted as has been shown by us, in the later dramas, the similarity of Prakrit ceases to be of any significance. If in a drama written today Prakrit such as is found in *Sakuntala* is adopted, that would not take away from *Sakuntala* its antiquity. And further we do not argue that the Prakrit is ancient and therefore *Bhasa* must be its author but that *Bhasa* is the author and the Prakrit accordingly ancient. Therefore all arguments of the other side based on the Prakrit are in vain.

V. Then the Pisharodis say that the varying merits of the dramas is another point against *Bhasa's* authorship and cite *Svapnavasavdatta* and *Pratijnayaugandharayana* by way of illustration.

We can only regard all this as unrestrained expressions of opinions formed by them most gratuituouly. For, with the object of establishing that many authors jointly compiled the dramas they boldly state it as their *ipse dixit* that in one drama the style is artificial and in another natural, that in the same drama the style in one act is of one kind while it is different in another act, that in the same drama the merits vary with the several acts and so on. But all these statements are left undemonstrated.

The Pisharodis freely dogmatise without logically supporting their statements, and why do they not argue in the same strain that the merits of the dramas like *Vikramorvasiya* vary from act to act, and therefore they should have been compiled by several authors? .

In fact everyone of these dramas displays the same charming evolution of plot in a setting of several apt and varied incidents, appropriate situations and measured expression of the human sentiments as interacted by them, richness of sound and sense in consonance with the sentiments and feelings portrayed, working out of the *sandhis* and *Sandhyangas* as required, and universal flow, as it were, of the Rasas; from which it can be inferred as in the case of *Sakuntala* and its connected works that they must all have emanated from the genius of one author. The critics who read these dramas well can themselves appreciate all these qualities; they have also been set forth by us in brief and *in extenso* in our introductions to *Pratima* and others; and they can also be grasped by reading our commentaries on *Svapnavasavadatta* and the rest. In short these dramas should be reckoned the very best ornaments of the Sanskrit literature, and among them *Svapnavasavadatta* and *Pratima* the very crown jewels. So it stands.

The argument of the Pisharodis that because the merits of the dramas vary, they should have been compiled by several authors, is answered by this consideration that the difference in the Rasa and Bhava must necessarily produce a corresponding difference in style and substance

Then the Pisharodis say that we emphasise two of the characteristics in these dramas—the statement "नान्द्यन्ते ततः प्रविशति सूत्रधारः" and the use of the word Sthapana at the end of the Prastavana as distinguishing features of Bhasa's dramas.

From this it appears that they have not carefully read our introduction to the *Svapnavasavadatta*. After establishing by other and unexceptionable reasons which independently support the conclusion that *Bhasa* must have been the author of these dramas, we added that the opening of the drama with the *Sutradhara* might also be taken as a distinguishing feature. Nor does the fact that this feature, which was favoured by *Bhasa*, the foremost among poets, was adopted by his later successors, in any way detract from his position as the first among poets.

Then it is said that in the drama called *Ascharya-chudamani* written by *Saktibhadra* of Kerala, the play begins with "नान्द्यन्ते ततः प्रविशति सूत्रधारः" in the *Prastavana* we find the sentences "मयि विज्ञापनव्यग्रे शब्द इव श्रूयते। अङ्ग! पश्यामि।" and it concludes with the word *Sthapna*—features found in the *Svapna* group of dramas. It is also based on *Kalidasa's* works.

The only conclusion that follows from this is that *Saktibhadra* of Kerala relished the *Svapna* group of dramas so much that he deemed it a good fortune that his drama *Ascharyachuda-mani* should be modelled on them. That is a point against those who are anxious to detract from the merits of the *Svapna* group of dramas. The fact that that drama is based on *Kalidasa's* works only leads to this that it must be taken to be based on these dramas as well, for *Kalidasa's* works themselves are based on these dramas. The beginning of the drama with "नान्द्यन्ते ततः प्रविशति सूत्रधारः" and the mention of *Sthapana* are conventions of ancient dramas as witness the *Bhana* called *Ubhayabhisarika* written by sage *Vararuchi*. Therefore the praise of *Ascharyachudamani* and of its author is to no purpose and the attempt of the Pisharodis to found their argument on the *Prastavana* of that work is all of no avail.

VI. The conclusions to which the Pisharodis came as a result of their investigation is that these dramas are compilations made out of ancient works with a view to meet the large demands of the flourishing stage of Kerala. And they say that they are fortified in their conclusions by a hoary tradition to the effect that in ancient times there was a large amount of compilation work.

Our answer is this. We have repeatedly shown that the conclusions so far as they are based on their own personal investigation are incorrect. We have made it out that these dramas possessing the requisite and full number of acts must like *Sakuntala* and others have been original compositions not based on the works of others. Where then is the room for now doubting that they are only compilations? As for the tradition, that has evidently been set up by the other side so as to support its theory of compilation. For we have not come across any tradition in Kerala that Sanskrit dramas, complete with the requisite acts, were compilations. What all the Chakyar actors in Kerala did was that they selected from among the famous Sanskrit dramas such acts as they regarded as most beautiful and acted them with dress and technique after their own liking. Even now in some temples they depend on this for their livelihood. This matter has been already mentioned by us in page 79 *supra*.

Even assuming that there is such a tradition as the Pisharodis would have us believe, there is no evidence that these particular dramas were ever so compiled from other dramas. But from out of this *Svapna* group of dramas some acts of surpassing beauty were selected by these Chakyars, appropriately named and acted by them. They appear even in the list furnished by the Pisharodis (at page 112) of dramas stated to have been acted hereditarily in some Chakyar family, in the *Attaprakara*.

That list ought to be thus transcribed:—

1. Tapatisamvarana } Both, works of Kulasekhara
2. Dhananjaya } Varma
3. Nagananda of Sri Harsha
4. Ascharyachudamani of Saktibhadra
5. Kalyanasaugandhika of Nilakantha *

* The Pisharodis say that the name of the author of *Kalyanasaugandhika* is unknown. Evidently they have had no access to a complete copy of this single-act drama which is well-known and can be obtained everywhere in Kerala. In the *Sthapana*, the author's name is also menitoned. It is therefore surprising that persons who take so much interest in Kerala dramas should be ignorant of even the author's name.

6. Srikrishnacharita (not available)
7. Vichchhinnabhisheka (the 1st act of *Pratima*)
8. Sephalikanka and Svapnanka } They are the fourth and fifth acts of *Svapnavasavadatta*
9. Toranayuddham Valivadham } Both of the *Abhishekanataka*
10. Mallanka (the fourth act of *Balacharita*)
11. Mantranka (the third act of *Pratijnayaugandharayana*)
12. Dutavakya
13. Karnabhara
14. Dutaghatotkacha

In the above list the Pisharodis have written instead of 8 to 11 as given herein, *Svapnavasavadatta*, *Abhisheka*, *Balacharita* and *Pratijnayaugandharayana*; and the reason for this misdescription is not clear. *Vichchhinnabhisheka* is the first act of *Pratima*, in the same manner as *Sephalikanka*, *Svapnanka*, and the like. Now the Pisharodis proceed as if it were an original and independent drama and ascribe its authorship to Bhaskara Ravi Varman and for this, tradition is quoted as authority. But this tradition is known only to them and is of the same species as the other tradition mentioned before; and it is a convenient device to support the other side in its conclusions which lack every foundation. It is unnecessary to further expatiate on this, as it is impossible to attribute the authorship of *Vischchhinnabhisheka* which really means *Pratima* to any writer who is not older than *Kalidasa*.

VII. (a). The Pisharodis further say that the omission of the poet's name in the *Prastavana* is not due to the convention of those days but to the fact that it was impossible to scribe any one poet's authorship to the dramas which were compiled piecemeal by several authors.

This has been answered in repelling the theory that the several acts of these dramas were severally composed. And while the Pisharodis have made mighty efforts at establishing that in the dramas extending over a plurality of acts, there has been a plurality of authorship, none such has been shown as regards the single-act drama like *Madhyamavyayoga*, such as that the various stanzas and sentences were composed by distinct authors. And thus when it becomes established that they were the works of one hand, why was the author's name which ought to have surely been there mentioned, omitted? What is the answer of the Pisharodis to this? They have, however, reluctantly to admit that the dramas like *Madhyamavyayoga* must have been composed before the practice arose of mentioning the author's name in the prologue. And when we come so far, it is but proper to admit that the connected *Svapna* group of dramas exhibiting the like qualities are also of the same authorship. This convention of not mentioning the author's name is also seen elsewhere in a drama anterior to *Kalidasa*. That is the *Bhana* called *Ubhayabhisarika* written by sage *Vararuchi*. There neither the name of the poet nor of the drama is mentioned in the *Sthapana* but at the end of the work is to be found transcribed "Thus ends the *Bhana* called *Ubhayabhisarika* composed by sage *Vararuchi*" § In our plays the name of the dramas is written at the end but not the author's name. That is the only difference. From this it is easy to see how the name of the poet who wrote these dramas came to be forgotten and how he must be older than even sage *Vararuchi*.

(b) The next argument of the Pisharodis is this. In the *Lochana* of *Abhinavaguptacharya* the verse स्वाक्षितपक्ष्मकवाटं नयनद्वारं is quoted as from *Svapnavasavadatta* and it is not found in the *Svapnavasavadatta* comprised in this group of dramas. This argues the existence of another *Svapnavasavadatta* which may be the original of the present drama.

We ask——is this so-called original *Svapnavasavadatta* of the same story and plot as the present *Svapnavasavadatta* or of a different story and plot describing mainly the marriage of *Vasavadatta*? In the first view, this stanza, describing as

§ "इति वररुचिमुनिकृतिरुभयाभिसारिका नाम भाणः समाप्तः ॥"

it does the first stages of love freshly formed towards the king could not find place even in the so-called original *Svapnavasavadatta*, as has been pointed by us before.* In the second view even though such a stanza could find a place in a *Svapnavasavadatta* of a different kind, that drama cannot, for the very reason, be the basis of the present one. In either view therefore this theory of a suppositious original *Svapnavasavadatta* must be given up.

Thus the very *Svapnavasavadatta* found in this group of dramas must be the composition of sage *Bhasa*. It is not correct to postulate the existence of another *Svapnavasavadatta*. If a stanza or two be quoted as from *Svapnavasavadatta* and be not found here, then, if they cannot fit in with the context, it must be supposed that the person who so quoted made a mistake in the name of the work because the stanza cannot possibly be there; but if it can fit in with the context, then we must suppose that there must be clerical † omission in the manuscripts by reason of their not having been current for a long time and this because it is a certainty that they must have been there. When we find some portions missing in the manuscripts even of widely read works § is it surprising that this should occur in works which have long ceased to be in vogue? This then is the position most satisfactory and unattended by any difficulties and one which will commend itself to all right-minded and learned men. The forgoing also disproves the contention of Dr. Barnett who accepts the theory of the two Pisharodis.

As a result of all these discussions the conclusion becomes finally established that *Bhasa* must have been the author of

---

* Pages 20 and 21 supra.

† Vide PP. 76 and 113 of the Svapnavasavadatta with commentary, 1924 edition.

§ For instance, the stanzas "नखलु नखलु बाणः सन्निपात्योऽयमस्मिन्", "कुल्याम्भोभिः पवनचपलैः", in Sakuntala 1st Act are not found in the Nirnayasagar edition.

Svapnavasavadatta found in this group of dramas and that likewise he must have been the author of the other connected dramas as well.

In further prosecuting the search of records for *Svapnavasavadatta*, I have now fortunately obtained documentary authority in support of my position. *Bhavaprakasa* is, it is well-known, a work on Rhetoric written in the 12th century A. D. by *Saradatanaya* and accepted as authority by *Vidyanatha* and others. There, in the 8th Adhikara, in dealing with the features of the ten kinds of Rupakas after describing the five Jatis mentioned by *Subandhu*, viz, Purna, Prasanta, Bhasvara, Lalita, and Samagra, the author says:—

"प्रशान्तरसभूयिष्ठं प्रशान्तं नाम नाटकम् ।
न्यासो न्याससमुद्भेदो बीजोक्तिर्बीजदर्शनम् ॥
ततोऽनुद्दिष्टसंहारः प्रशान्ते पञ्च सन्धयः ।
सात्वती वृत्तिरत्र स्यादिति द्रौहिणिरब्रवीत् ॥
स्वप्नवासवदत्ताख्यमुदाहरणमत्र तु ।
आच्छिद्य भूपाद् व्यसनाद् देवी मागधिकाकरे ॥
न्यस्ता यतस्ततो (स्यास्य ? न्यासाद्) मुखसन्धिरयं भवेत् ।
न्यासस्य च प्रतिमुखं समुद्भेद उदाहृतम् ॥
(a) पद्मावत्या मुखं वीक्ष्य विशेषकविभूषितम् ।
जीवत्यावन्तिकेस्येतद् ज्ञातं भूमिभुजा यथा ॥
उत्कण्ठितेन सोद्वेगं बीजोक्तिर्नामकीर्तनम् ।
एहि वासवदत्तेति (?) क्वयासीत्यादि दृश्यते ॥
सहावास्थितयोरेकं प्राप्यान्यस्य गवेषणम् ।
दर्शनस्पर्शनालापैरेतत् स्याद् बीजदर्शनम् ॥
(अत्रोदाहरणं) —

(a) For this sloka, refer to Svapnavasavadatta with commentary p. 118, 1924 edition.

चिरप्रसुप्तः कामो मे वीणया प्रतिबोधितः ।
तां तु देवीं न पश्यामि यस्या घोषवती प्रिया ॥
किं ते भूयः प्रियं कुर्यामितिवाग् यत्र नोच्यते ।
तमनुद्दिष्टसंहारमित्याहुर्भरतादयः ॥"

These passages show that *Vasavadatta* was separated from *Vatsaraja* and entrusted to *Padmavati* (as in the first act), that *Vatsaraja* believed that *Vasavadatta* was alive (vide 5th act), that the king feelingly called for *Vasavadatta*, by name and so on (as in the fifth act) and that the king having got *Ghoshavati* (वीणा) searched for *Vasavadatta* its possessor (vide 6th act), all as in the *Svapnavasavadatta*; and further the verse "चिरप्रसुप्तः कामो मे वीणया प्रतिबोधितः" found in the sixthact is actually quoted.

Moreover in the *Sringaraprakasa* of *Bhojadeva* who lived in the 11th century, a work on Rhetoric, accepted as authority by *Vidyadhara*, author of *Ekavali*, the *Svapnavasavadatta* is mentioned by name and the plot of the fifth act is thus described:—

"स्वप्नवासवदत्ते पद्मावतीमस्वस्थां द्रष्टुं राजा समुद्रगृहकं गतः । पद्मावतीरहितं च तदवलोक्य तस्या एव शयनीये सुष्वाप । वासवदत्तां च स्वप्नवदस्वप्ने ददर्श । स्वप्नायमानश्च वासवदत्तामाबभाषे । स्वप्नशब्देन चेह स्वापो वा स्वप्नदर्शनं वा स्वप्नायितं वा विवक्षितम् ॥"

(12th Prakasa of the *Sringaraprakasa*.)

What greater authority is required than what is furnished by these two writings, *Bhavaprakasa* and *Sringaraprakasa*? Had I obtained these before, there would not have been the slightest discussion over my view that *Bhasa* should have been the author of this *Svapnavasavadatta*. Luckily my opinion has now been vindicated.

(e) Some other doubts regarding Bhasa's authorship.

A Scholar recently wrote to me raising some doubts in regard to *Bhasa's* authorship of the plays They are:—

1. the stanzas embodied in the *Subhashitavali* and other anthologies ascribing them to *Bhasa* are not found in the *Svapnavasavadatta* and other plays ;

2. the passages quoted in other works as from the *Svapnavasavadatta* are not found in the manuscripts now obtained ;

3. the sloka पद्मावत्या मुखं वीक्ष्य विशेषकविभूषितम् । etc quoted in the *Bhavaprakasa* as belonging to the *Svapnavasavadatta* (vide page 113 of 1924 edition) does not fit in the text in the same form ; and

4. the quotations from the *Sakuntala* exist in all the maunscripts of the work, while two slokas quoted as from the *Svapnavasavadatta* are not found in the available manuscripts of the work ; hence the inappropriateness in taking *Sakuntala* as an illustration of the *Svapnavasavadatta*.

The first objection has already been met (vide page 81 *supra*).

Regarding the second objection, there are altogether three slokas which are quotations from the *Svapnavasavadatta*, * one in the *Natyadarpana*, and § two in the *Bhavaprakasa*. A part of the story of the *Svapnavasavadatta* is also found summarised in the *Sringaraprakasa*. All these, it would be noted can find suitable places in the text. This has been fully explained in my commentary on the *Savpnavasavadatta*, 1924 edition. Even among the quotations in the *Natyadarpana* and *Bhavaprakasa*, only two slokas पादाक्रान्तानि पुष्पाणि and पद्मावत्या मुखं वीक्ष्य are missing in the available manuscripts

* "पादाक्रान्तानि पुष्पाणि सोष्म चेदं शिलातलम् । नूनं काचिदिहासीना मां दृष्ट्वा सहसा गता ॥" (स्वप्न. p. 76). § "पद्मावत्या मुखं वीक्ष्य विशेषकविभूषितम् । जीवत्यावन्तिकेत्येतत् पूर्वं विज्ञातमेव मे ॥" (स्वप्न. p. 113) "चिरप्रसुप्तः कामो मे वीणया प्रतिबोधितः । तां तु देवीं न पश्यामि यस्या घोषवती प्रिया ॥" (स्वप्न. p. 124).

of the *Svapnavasavadatta* and the reason why they are missing is also explained in pages 76 and 113 of the above mentioned edition.

As to the third objection, it should be said that it is only proper that the sloka 'पद्मावत्या मुखं वीक्ष्य विशेषकविभूषितम् । जीवत्यावन्तिकेत्येतद् ज्ञातं भूमिभुजायथा ॥' which is an illustration does not fit in the *Svapnavasavadatta* in the form in which it appears in the *Bhavaprakasa*. For, the author of the *Bhavaprakasa* adopting a part of the sense of the sloka "पद्मावत्या मुखं वीक्ष्य विशेषकविभूषितम् । जीवत्यावन्तिकेत्येतत् पूर्वं विज्ञातमेव मे" in the same words, shows न्यायसमुद्भेद in the illustration in his own words "ज्ञातं भूमिभुजा यथा". The words ज्ञातं भूमिभुजा यथा must necessarily be those of the author quoting, just as the latter half of the sloka

"लिम्पतीव तमोऽङ्गानि वर्षतीवाञ्जनं नभः ।
इतीदमपि भूयिष्ठमुत्प्रेक्षालक्षणान्वितम् ॥"

in *Kavyadarsa*, is *Dandin's* own showing the definition of उत्प्रेक्षा in the illustration—

"लिम्पतीव तमोऽङ्गानि वर्षतीवाञ्जनं नभः ।
असत्पुरुषसेवेव दृष्टिर्निष्फलतां गता ॥"

There is however a slight distinction. While, in the *Kavyadarsa*, a part of the sloka itself is quoted, in the *Bhavaprakasa*, a part of the sense only of a sloka is adapted. *Dandin* uses the word इति in इतीदं etc. which shows the portion of the sloka preceding it to be a quotation while the author of the *Bhavprakasa* indicates that he has derived a part of the sense without using इति but by changing the last four words of the sloka. When the words of the king in the sloka is in the following form—

पद्मावत्या मुखं वीक्ष्य विशेषकविभूषितम् ।
जीवत्यावन्तिकेत्येवत् पूर्वं विज्ञातमेव मे ॥

a major portion of the sense will become borrowed by the substitution of the three words ज्ञातं भूमिभुजा यथा for the four words पूर्वं विज्ञातम् एव मे and the न्यासमुद्भेद also aptly illustrated. Hence the sloka in the *Bhavaprakasa* is naturally not in its perfect form.

With regard to the fourth objection, it may be remarked that even though all the quotations from the *Sakuntala* are traced in all the manuscripts of the work, even though all the quotations from the *Svapnavasavadatta* are not to be found in the manuscripts so far obtained, nothing is lost thereby. For, just as two stanzas missing in certain manuscripts of the *Sakuntala* are found in others, so the two slokas from the *Svapnavasavadatta* which do not occur in the manuscripts now available may be found in fresh manuscripts that may yet be discovered. What is meant by the foregoing is that in respect of certain slokas existing in a particular manuscript but not in others, the *Svapnavasavadatta* compares favourably with the *Sakuntala* and this comparison does not stand contradicted either by the fact that all the quotations from the *Sakuntala* can be traced in all the manuscripts of the work or by the fact that the slokas cited as from the *Savpnavasavadatta* are not found in the available manuscripts.

Besides, it is quite proper that all the *Sakuntala* quotations are traced while the *Svapnavasavadatta* quotations are not. The non-existence in the manuscripts of certain slokas and prose-passages that are cited by authors of note might very well have been the result of copyist's omission to write them down. Such omission in the case of a work that is in large circulation may be soon rectified by students and teachers who would naturally be anxious to have perfect copies by collecting different manuscript copies that may be available. It may therefore be said that, generally, works that are widely read contain few or no omissions. On the other hand, works that have long ceased from circulaion invariably contain omissions which have not the least chance of rectification because they are very seldom used for study and also because sufficient number of manuscript copies may not be available. The *Sakuntala* is an exceedingly popular work and very widely read and therefore, manuscript copies of the work can be obtained in crores. There is thus no possibility of that work containing omissions. The *Svapnavasavadatta* on the other hand, has for many centuries past ceased from circulation and only seven or eight manuscript copies of it still linger. And even these might have been copied from imperfect original. Such being the case, the absence of one or two slokas and prose-bits in the manuscripts of the *Svapnavasavadatta* which occur as quotations in works on poetics, has to be attributed to the want of circulation of the work. Thus when there is a legitimate argument for the absence in the *Svapnavasavadatta* of a few quotations, there is no necessity for a far-fetched surmise that there may be another *Svapnavasvadatta* which we do not know.

The foregoing discussion negatives also the * contention of Professor Sylvain Levi who, quoting the passage "भासकृते स्वप्नवासवदत्ते..." from the *Natyadarpana* says that the Trivandrum *Svapnavasavadatta* is not the work of *Bhasa*, as the sloka quoted in the *Natyadarpana* as from *Bhasa's Svapnavasavadatta* is not found in it. For, the absence of slokas might very well be explained as due to copyists' omissions. We have also shown that, for the sloka quoted in the *Natyadarpana*, there is an appropriate place in the fourth act of the *Svapnavasavadatta* after 'उभावुपविशतः' (P. 76, 1924 edition).

Professor Levi observes that the phrase भासकृते in the passage भासकृते स्वप्नवासवदत्ते in the *Natyadarpana* indicates the existence of another *Svapnavasavadatta* written by a poet other than *Bhasa*. Here we ask——is the *Svapnavasavadatta* distinguished by him as written by *Bhasa* an established one or not? If it is the latter, the phrase भासकृते would only serve the same purpose as the word "fragrant" (सुरभि) serves

* (Vide Journal Asiatique for October—December 1923.)

"sky-lotus." (गगनारविन्दं). Hence the other alternative only has to be accepted; in which case, the established *Svapnavasavadatta* must be the one discovered by us and distinctly bearing the name *Svapnavasavadatta*. The phrase भासकृते is purely of a descriptive character; it does not distinguish the *Svapnavasavadatta* of *Bhasa* from another work of the same name. Nor can it be inferred from the non-existence of one or two slokas in the discovered manuscripts of the *Svapnavasavadatta* that there must be another *Svapnavasavadatta* containing them; for, they might have been omitted by copyists. Similar omission by copyists of one or two slokas or addition of one or two slokas in some of the manuscripts of the *Sakuntala*, will not, we think, lead one to infer that there may be several *Sakuntalas* written by several authors. For the same reason, the statement that the published *Svapnavasavadatta* might be an easy adaptation of a bigger original work becomes of no value. Futher, it cannot be denied that a vigorous style and clear diction and similar other characteristics common in the original works of master poets run throughout the published *Svapnavasavadatta* as in the *Sakuntala* and other great works.

It may be asked, if there is only one *Svapnavasavadatta* just as there is only one *Sakuntala*, why should the author of the *Natyadarpana* qualify the word स्वप्नवासवदत्ते by भासकृते ? Would it not be sufficient on his part to state merely यथा स्वप्नवासवदत्ते like यथा शाकुन्तले, यथा रत्नावल्याम् etc ? We have already said that the phrase भासकृते in यथा भासकृते स्वप्नवासवदत्ते is of a descriptive and not distinguishing character. Such phrases are not uncommon in Sanskrit literature; e. g.

'यथा मङ्खीये श्रीकण्ठस्तवे' (अलङ्कारसर्वस्वे)

'गुणकिरणावल्यामुदयनाचार्यैरुदितम्' (दिनकरभट्टीये)

'यदुक्तं न्यायकुसुमाञ्जलावुदयनाचार्यैः' (साहित्यदर्पणे)

'यथा लक्ष्म्यङ्कता किराते भारवेः' (हेमचन्द्रकाव्यानुशासने)

'तथा चाश्वचरिते वसन्तराजः' (अमरकोशटीकासर्वस्वे)

'उपाध्यायसर्वस्वे दामोदरेणोक्तम्')

If it is still persisted that the author of the *Natyadarpana* would not have used it aimlessly, we would refer to the*article by Dr. Thomas where he suggests that the phrase is used with the object of informing the readers of the name of the author of the verse quoted, who might otherwise be ignorant of it. This is especially necessary in the case of the *Svapnavasavadatta*. When a verse or a prose passage is found quoted in a work, it would naturally stir the curiosity of the reader to know the source of the quotation as well as its author. To satisfy this curiosity, it is the duty of the writer quoting to mention the source and its author. But when the name of a work that plainly mentions the name of its author within the body, is given, it is not necessary to mention also the name of the author because it can well be ascertained from a perusal of the work itself. For instance, when the name of the *Sakuntala* is mentioned it is not necessary to give the name of its author also, as it is found in the prelude to that work itself. On the other hand, when mentioning a work in which the name of the author is not given it is quite necessary that it should be mentioned along with the name of the work, as otherwise there is no means of knowing it. Acting up to this principle, the author of the *Natyadarpana* having in mind that the name of author is not mentioned in the prelude to the *Svapnavasavadatta* and that, therefore, the readers should be informed of it, qualifies स्वप्नवासवदत्ते by भासकृते. What we say is that the author of the *Natyadarpana*, by qualifying स्वप्नवासवदत्ते by भासकृते and thereby indicating that the *Svapnavasavadatta* of *Bhasa* does not reveal its author's name in the prelude, clearly shows that he thinks of the *Svapnavasavadatta* published by us,

It will thus be seen that in the realm of Sanskrit literature there is only one drama of the name of *Svapnavasavadatta* and that by *Bhasa*; and it is certain that it is the one published by us. In this connection, it is well to remember what we said regarding the three distinguishing marks of *Bhasa's Svapnavasavadatta* (P. 87 supra).

---

* Vide J. R, A. S. of Great Britain and Ireland for January 1925.

Prof. Levi also quotes another passage from the *Natakalakshanaratnakosa* by *Sagaranandin* which reads as follows:-

"यथा स्वप्नवासवदत्ते, नेपथ्ये सूत्रधारः (उत्सारणां श्रुत्वा पठति) अये कथं तपोवनेऽप्युत्सारणा। (विलोक्य) कथं मन्त्री यौगन्धरायणो वत्सराजस्य राज्यप्रत्यानयनं कर्तुकामः पद्मावतीयजनेनोत्सार्यते । इत्युत्सारणाशब्दोऽत्र पूर्वकप्रयोगमुत्सार्य नाटकार्थसूचक इति प्रयोगातिशयः"

This is not found in the published *Svapnavasavadatta* and in its place a different passage occurs. Hence the work now published is not the genuine *Svapnavasavadatta* of *Bhasa*. We shall now deal with this point.

Prof. Levi thinks that, in the above passage, the portion from the word अये up to उत्सार्यते is the speech of the *Sutradhara* quoted by *Sagaranandin* from the *Svapnavasavadatta*. But we are of opinion that this passage is only an expansion, in *Sagaranandin's* own words, of the sloka

"भवतु विज्ञातं—भृत्यैर्मगधराजस्य स्निग्धैः कन्यानुगामिभिः ।
धृष्टमुत्सार्यते सर्वस्तपोवनगतो जनः ॥"

found in the prelude of the published drama and spoken by the *Sutradhara* after hearing उत्सारणशब्द behind the scene. For, in doing so, the sense conveyed by the suggestive words of the *Sutradhara* will have been fully explained. The purport of the passage is this: —"In the *Svapnavasavadatta*, the *Sutradhara*, having heard the voice of the servants in turning the people away, gets anxious to know how there could be any exercise of authority in an Asrama which is not the proper place for it and, looking towards the quarter where he could find out the reason for this unbecoming act, exclaims that the minister *Yaugandharayana*, who is on the mission of recovering the lost kingdom of the *Vatsaraja*, is being turned away by the servants of *Padmavati*". This sense will become clearer if the word इति is put after उत्सारणा; and it may be that it has been omitted by mistake by copyists. The passage cited by Prof. Levi has therefore to be reset thus:—

"यथा स्वप्नवासवदत्ते नेपथ्ये सूत्रधारः उत्सारणां श्रुत्वा पठति अये कथं तपोवनेऽप्युत्सारणा (इति) विलोक्य,—कथं मन्त्री यौगन्धरायणो वत्सराजस्य राज्यप्रत्यापनयनं कर्तुकामः पद्मावतीयजनेनोत्सार्यते इति। उत्सारणाशब्दोऽत्र पूर्वकप्रयोगमुत्थाप्य नाटककार्यसूचक इति प्रयोगातिशयः।"

Now it might be asked why the portion from अये कथम् up to उत्सार्यते should not be taken as the direct utterance of the *Sutradhara* as is done by Prof. Levi. The reason is that, in that case, that portion should have to be taken as issueing from the mouth of *Bhasa* himself. This is obviously impossible, as the passage not only lacks the dignity of sense and expression common in the utterances of Mahakavis but also contains the dry expressions common among commentators. The component word पद्मावतीय in पद्मावतीयजनेन, especially, is used in the sense of "servants belonging to *Padmavati*"; but it should be noted that not even a poetaster, much less an eminent poet like *Bhasa* who stands as a model even to *Kalidasa*, would choose the word पद्मावती with the termination ईय affixed to it in a prose passage unfettered by metrical rules, when it is quite open for him to use the simple word पद्मावतीजनेन or पद्मावतीपरिजनेन without the ईय termination. In the prose passages of a commentary, however, in which the beauties of a Kavya are not expected, an author may use the word with ईय termination with a view to bring out the relationship (सम्बन्ध); e. g., पर्वतीयबर्हिः, चत्वरीयबर्हिः etc. That the verse of the *Sutradhara* in the published *Svapnavasavadatta* is of a high order both in sound and sense will be clear to all readers. This is explained fully in our commentary. It is therefore correct to say that the verse,

'भृत्यैर्मगधराजस्य स्निग्धैः कन्यानुगामिभिः।
धृष्टमुत्सार्यते सर्वस्तपोवनगतो जनः॥'

is *Bhasa's* own.

The above discussion answers also the article * of Dr. Barnett who repeats the arguments of Prof. Levi for the theory

* Pp. 519-522 Vol. III Bulletin of the School of Oriental Studies, London.

of the existence of more than one *Svapnavasavadatta*. In the same article, Dr. Barnett makes some statements while criticising the arguments of Dr. Keith. We shall now take up the following which call for our consideration.

(1). Dr. Barnett observes that arguments from style depends on subjective taste. It is not clear to us what this proves for him. This much is sure, that Gunas inherent in expressions, sentiments and emotions vary according to the merits of a Kavya and that it determines the degree of literary excellence in a work. That is why we argued that the *Svapna* group of plays surpass the plays of *Kalidasa* and we think that it is for the same reason that Drs. Keith, Thomas, Winternitz, Stenkonow and other scholars intensely admire them.

(2) Dr. Barnett says that grammatical archaisms are a common technique of the Kerala playwrights. We do not know on what authority his statement is based. But the statement implies the charge that the Kerala writers are careless with regard to grammatical accuracy. This is wrong †. I have had to acquaint myself with almost all the works of the Kerala writers and I know fully well the features common to them. They are strict followers of *Panini's* school of grammar and averse to grammatical soleoisms. This will be evident to all from a perusal of the Keraliya works published in the Trivandrum Sanskrit Series.

(3) Dr. Keith rightly remarks that the *Nyayasastra* of *Medhatithi* mentioned in the *Pratimanataka* cannot be the *Manubhashya* of *Medhatithi*, for, the *Manubhashya* does not in reality differ from the *Manudharmasastra* already mentioned as मानवीयं धर्मशास्त्रम् and it would be improper for *Ravana* who claims proficiency in several branches of learning to repeat a sastra once mentioned. Dr. Barnett objects this by saying that it is possible that the *Manubhashya* is mentioned

† Dr. Barnett's implied charge is of the same kind as that of the Pisharodis exposed in page 101 supra.

separately from the *Manudharmasastra* just as the *Nirukta*, (which is in fact a commentary on the *Veda*), is mentioned separately from the *Veda* in the *Mahabharata*. This argument is not correct. The *Nirukta* is only a part (अङ्ग) of the Veda, the whole (अङ्गि). It is therefore proper to mention the part just after the whole. But the *Manubhashya* does not stand on any such relationship with the *Manudharmasastra*. Futher, the *Nyayasastra* of *Medhatithi* is not mentioned next to the *Manudharmasastra* but only after two other different sastras viz, the *Yogasastra* and the *Arthasastra*. Besides, one would expect that a person like *Ravana* should refer to the works of very ancient authors of divine or semi-divine origin and not to the writings of comparatively recent writers like *Medhatithi*, *Nandanasuri*, *Kullukabhatta* and others. Hence, the *Medhatithi* mentioned in the *Pratima* must be the Rishi referred to in the *Veda* by that name,

(4) As the discovered plays show differences in style, argues Dr. Barnett, they are not written by one and the same author. This cannot stand. Various Rasas are embodied in the plays and the style must needs vary so as to suit the various Rasas. For instance, the style adopted in a love drama will hardly suit a heroic drama. In Kavyas, therefore, the various styles adopted to suit the various Rasas are not opposed to their being written by one author. Then what is it that indicates the hand of the same author in a group of works? It is the equality of thought and the description of the same thoughts as well as the mentioning of the same verse or prose or a part thereof in two or more works. All these are found in plenty in the *Svapna* group. With regard to the three features in these plays, namely (1) that they begin with the entry of the *Sutradhara*, (2) that the word *Sthapana* is used in the place of *Prastavana* and (3) that neither the name of the work nor the name of author is mentioned in them, we referred to them not to prove the singleness of authorship but to show that these features are not generally met

with in dramas. It is with this idea that we said in our introduction to the *Svapnavasavadatta*, "These natakas are thus seen to be the works of *Bhasa* as the epithet, सूत्रधारकृतारम्भैः, by which *Bhatta Bana* qualifies *Bhasa's* natakas, applies to these plays, for every one of them begins with the stage direction, नान्द्यन्ते ततः प्रविशति सूत्रधारः।" Our opinion is this—that since *Bhasa* is a pioneer in the field of Sanskrit dramas, the opening of the plays with the entrance of the *Sutradhara* in his plays can be taken to be his own invention and for that reason it can also be considered as a special feature of his dramas. That later playwrights imitating *Bhasa* have adapted this feature in their plays, is a different matter. From what we have explained above, it will be seen that another objection of Dr. Barnett that the comedy भगवदज्जुकीय which possesses all the three features enumerated already, will have to be accepted as written by *Bhasa*, is removed. Whether that high-class comedy is also a work of *Bhasa* or of some other poet, we hope to discuss at length when we publish the work.

(5) Dr. Barnett says* that there are grounds to doubt whether the *Svapnavasavadatta* mentioned in the *Bhavaprakasa* is the same as the one published by us. But for our part we find ample evidence to convince us that it is the published *Svapnavasavadatta* that is mentioned in the *Bhavaprakasa*. It is that *Bhavaprakasa* speaks of six matters as occurring in the *Svapnavasavadatta*. They are:—(1) the separation of *Vasavadatta* from *Udayana* under the pretext of व्यसन (burning the village) and placing her as a trust in the hands of *Padmavati*, (2) the inference of *Udayana* from the beautiful तिलक in *Padmavati's* face that *Vasavadatta* was alive, (3) the exclaiming of the name of *Vasavadatta* by *Udayana* out of deep sorrow for her, (4) *Udayana* having procured the musical instrument, Vina, his search for its bosom companion, *Vasavadatta*, and his talks on the matter, (5) the illustration of the sloka expressed by *Udayana*, viz, चिरप्रसुप्तः कामो मे (which actually exists in the fifth act of our *Svapnavasavadatta*) and (6) the non-mention of such sayings as किं ते भूयः प्रियमुपहरामि at the close of the drama. All these

* P. 99, J. R. A. S of Great Britain and Ireland for January 1925.

matters are found in our *Svapnavasavadatta*. Even in regard to the portion relating to the inference of *Udayana* that *Vasavadatta* was alive, which might be an omission in the discovered manuscripts, we have shown in page 113 of our edition of the work with commentary published in 1924 that there is an appropriate and agreeable place for it in the fifth act. Above all, from the portions summarised in the *Sringaraprakasa* by Bhojadeva who flourished in the 11th cent. A. D., from the fifth act of the *Svapnavasavadatta*, it is certain that he has in mind the *Svapnavasavadatta* we have published.

We think that *Bhasa*, the author of these plays, was not merely older than *Asvaghosha* who lived in

(1) Dr. Sukthankar.

the first century A. D., and *Chanakya* who lived in the fourth century B. C., but older even than *Panini* who lived before them. And we will state our reasons for this. We have already met the various objections which have been urged against the priority of *Bhasa* to *Asvaghosha* and *Kautalya*. There remains only the objection of Dr. Sukthankar who, disputing the priority of *Bhasa* to *Panini*, says in Vol. 12 of the Journal of the Americal Oriental Society, that the priority of *Bhasa* to *Panini* could not be inferred from the use of archaic grammar and idioms of *Bhasa*, because such archaic expressions are to be found elsewhere also. Taking the archaic expressions, which are 27 in number, he thinks that 24 out of them are ordinary lapses from correct grammar and that 3 alone are extraordinary lapses. And even the 24 are shown to be ordinary only by showing similar lapses in the *Ramayana* and *Mahabharata* and not in the works of *Kalidasa* and such other writers; so that when it is argued that the archaic expressions of *Bhasa* are not peculiar to him, it must be understood that such expressions are to be found only in the *Ramayana* and *Mahabharata* and not in other works. And that is the very thing which we have been saying over and over again, viz., that in these as in the *Mahabharata* and *Ramayana* there is not to be found that strict adherence to *Panini* which is to be found in the writings of *Kalidasa* and others. For out of the 27 archaic forms shown in the list, excluding 11, 12, 19, 20 and 22, the others are nowhere to be found in the works of *Kalidasa*. And just as we say that the

Ramayana and *Mahabharata*, which stories are referred to in *Kautalya's Arthasastra*, are anterior to *Panini* because they do not conform to *Panini's* rules, so we say that *Bhasa* whose stanza from the *Pratijnayaugandharayana* is quoted by *Chanakya*, is also older than *Panini* to whose rules he does not conform either; or at least that *Bhasa* and *Panini* were nearly contemporaries. For it cannot be that a writer could so lightly disregard all *Panini*'s rules, as does *Bhasa* in his dramas, after the said rules had come into general vogue, as they did from the fourth century B. C. and at the same time command so much respect from *Kalidasa* and others who were such great admirers of *Panini*. But if it be said that *Kalidasa* and others had great regard for *Bhasa's* dramas, because of their antiquity, then that establishes our case. So we are not much impressed by the arguments of Dr. Sukthankar based on the use of archaic expressions in *Bhasa*. And it has already been shown that the mention of *Sakya–Sramanaka* in the *Charudatta* etc., does not militate against the priority of *Bhasa* to *Panini*. Even the number of archaic expressions in the works of *Bhasa* is not 27 as Dr. Sukthankar has mentioned, but a great deal more as will be evident from Appendix I.

And then, a writer says that King Darsaka mentioned in the *Svapnavasavadatta* is the same as the king Darsaka mentioned in the 99th chapter of *Vayupurana* as the father of Udayin who made Pataliputra his capital and as the son of Bimbisara who lived about 475 B. C. This is wrong; because *Bhasa* mentions Darsaka as contemporaneous with Pradyota, son of Palak, whereas the Vayu mentions Darsaka as the 12th King after Pradyota. Therefore the Darsaka of *Bhasa* must have been very much older than the Darsaka of the Vayu. It should not be doubted that the Pradyota of *Bhasa* might be different from the Pradyota of the Vayu because in *Bhasa* he is mentioned as the father of Gopalaka who is the same as Palaka mentioned in the Vayu as the son of Pradyota.

And another writer says that *Bhasa* must be later than Udayin because it was Udayin who converted the village of Patali into his capital and gave it the name of Pataliputra and

Bhasa refers to Pataliputra in the *Charudatta* in the passage पाटलीपुत्रं मे जन्मभूमिः. This is wrong; because there is nothing to show that before it was converted into capital it was not called Pataliputra; and also because the name simply means a place abounding in Patali flowers (or literally a place where Patalis are born) and this name would be appropriate whether the place was a village or a town or a metropolis.

And there is only this question which we want to put to Dr. Sukthankar, where did he get it that I said that *Charudatta* was a complete drama ‡ when as matter of fact we have stated in our introduction to the *Pratimanataka*, expressly and in so many words, that "the *Charudatta* is incomplete"?

41. The cause that led to the discovery of the manuscripts of the plays in Travancore and the conclusion.

It now remains for me to explain how this group of Rupakas happened to be unearthed for the first time in the Travancore State, Rupakas, shining as they are like the brilliants on the diadem of the ancient Natakas, furnishing a mine of information for researches in the field of ancient history, with perfection well worth imitation by all poets. The explanation is not far to seek; for, what led to our obtaining the *Purushakara*, the *Vyaktiviveka*, *Durghatavritti*, the *Jayamangala* and other works, already published and the *Bhoja-Vyakarana (Sarasvatikanthabharana)*, the *Natya-veda Vivriti*, the *Manjusri-Mulatantra* and other works, all very rare, applies to the Rupakas as well. From very ancient times, kings and nobilities of this land collected literary works with great effort, and preserved them in their residences. Even in these times, when Sanskrit has ceased to be wide-spread, their descendants do not generally show any indifference in preserving the manuscripts, though worn out and torn. This is why rare works are obtained in this State.

T. Ganapati Sastri.

—:o:—

‡ See the article in the Mythic Society Journal, April 1919.

APPENDIX I. ARCHAISMS IN BHASA'S WORKS.

[*The pages refer to the first edition of the plays.*]

भासरूपकगतानामार्षप्रयोगाणां सूचिका ।

———:o:———

प्रयोगाः	शास्त्राननुरोधप्रकारः ।
१. स्वस्ति भवते सपत्नीकाय (अवि. P. 108)	'प्रकृत्याशिषि' (6. 3. 83.) इति प्रकृतिभावविधिविरुद्धः समासः सहशब्दस्य सपत्नीकायेत्यत्र कृतः ।
२. काशिराजे (अवि. P. 110)	'राजाहःसखिभ्य' (5-4-91) इति समासान्तो न कृतः ।
३. सर्वराज्ञः (दूतवा. P. 82)	पूर्ववत् ।
४. व्यूढोराः (मध्य. P. 12)	उरःप्रभृतिभ्यः (5-4-151) इति कपा भाव्यम् ।
५. रुदन्तीम् (दूतवा. P. 33)	नुम् अशास्त्रीयः ।
६. गृह्य (दूतघ. P. 59)	ल्यप् शास्त्रविरुद्धः ।
७. मा दाणि भवं अणत्थं चिन्तिअ (स्वप्न. P. 60)	माशब्दयोगे क्त्वाप्रत्ययोऽशास्त्रीयः ।
८. मा मा भूयो अवहणिअ (स्वप्न. P. 32)	पूर्ववत् ।

९. मा णिब्बन्धिअ (अवि. P. 37) १०. अय्ये मा दार्णि अण्णं चिन्तिअ (स्वप्न. P. 25)	पूर्ववत् ।
११. मा दाणि भवं अत्ताणं ओहसिअं कादुं (स्वप्न. P. 59) १२. माखु माखु षाहषं कळिअ पविषदुं (बाल. P. 50) १३. माखु माखु भट्टा! एदं जळासअं पविसिदुं (बाल. P. 48) १४. माखु माखु मं शंविदुं (प्रतिज्ञा. P. 45) १५. मा दाणिं भट्टा! अदिमत्तं सन्ताप्पिदुं (स्वप्न. P. 69)	प्रतिषेधार्थोऽत्र माशब्दः । तद्योगे तु मुन् न विहितः ।
१६. जपापुष्पमिव रक्तलोचनः (प्रतिज्ञा. P. 56)	रक्तशब्दस्य सापेक्षत्वेऽपि समासः कृतः ।
१७. आपृच्छामि (स्वप्न. P. 15) १८. आपृच्छ (प्रतिमा. P. 81)	'आङ्नुप्रच्छयोः' (वार्त्ति० 1-3-21) इति आत्मनेपदेनैव भाव्यम् ।
१९. रक्षते (चारुद. P. 17)	आत्मनेपदमवैधम् ।
३०. छिद्यते २१. रुद्यते (स्वप्न. P. 69)	यगात्मनेपदे कर्तरि चिन्त्ये ।
२२. भ्रश्यते (प्रतिज्ञा. P. 8)	आत्मनेपदं चिन्त्यम् ।
२३. द्रक्ष्यते २४. भोष्यते (प्रतिज्ञा. P. 16)	यगात्मनेपदे कर्तरि चिन्त्ये ।

२५. पुत्रेति (बाल)	इह 'पुत्र इति' इति न्याय्ये सन्धिरशास्त्रीयः ।
२६. गमिष्ये (बाल. P. 67)	आत्मनेपदं कर्तरि चिन्त्यम् ।
२७. गर्जसे (बाल. P. 46) २८. स्त्रीगतां पृच्छसे कथाम् (पञ्च. P. 36) २९. पृच्छसे (प्रतिमा. P. 48)	आत्मनेपदमवैधम् ।
३०. रुध्यते (पञ्च. P. 37) ३१. शिष्यते (स्वप्न. P. 4)	परस्मैपदं न्याय्यम् ।
३२. वीजन्ति (अभिषे. P. 26) ३३. वीजन्तः (अभिषे. P. 26) ३४. समाश्वासितुम् (अभिषे. P. 68)	णिज्लोपोऽशास्त्रीयः ।
३५. उन्नामय (प्रतिमा. P. 66, 110)	ह्रस्व इह न कृतः उन्नमयेति हि भाव्यम् ।
३६. मे स्थापितः (प्रतिमा. P. 69)	पादादौ 'मे' आदेशो न विहितः । निपातत्वाश्रयणमगतिकगतिः ।
३७. उत्कण्ठिष्यति (स्वप्न. P. 16) ३८. परिष्वजति (अवि. P. 49) ३९. परिष्वज (अवि. P. 94) ४०. परिष्वजामि (बाल. P. 26) ४१. उपलप्स्यति (दूतघ. P. 54)	परस्मैपदमवैधम् । आत्मनेपदानित्यत्वं तु अगतिकगतिः ।
४२. प्रत्यायति (अभिषे. P. 24)	प्रत्याङ्पूर्वोऽयतिः प्रत्येतीत्यर्थेऽप्रसिद्धः । णिज्लोपाश्रयणे स एवावैधः ।

४३. विगाह्य उल्काम् (बाल. P. 22)	विसन्धिता दृश्यते ।
४४. ब्रह्मा ते हृदयम् (अभिषे. P. 73)	प्रथमपादान्ते लघोर्गुरुत्वं शार्दूलविक्रीडिते न प्रसिद्धम् ।
४५. अवन्त्याधिपतेः (स्वप्न. P. 54)	अधिपतिशब्दे आङः संश्लेषणमपूर्वम् । अवन्त्या अधिपतेरिति विवक्षणे सवर्णदीर्घोऽसाधुः ।
४६. यद्येवं नलागिरिग्रहणार्थं विमुक्तश्चेत् (प्रतिज्ञा. P. 70)	यदिशब्दचेच्छब्दयोः सहप्रयोगोऽप्रसिद्ध यदिः ।
४७. इष्टं चेदेकचित्तानां यद्यग्निः (अवि. P. 60)	पूर्ववत् ।
४८. यदि दातव्ये (पञ्च. P. 14)	यदिशब्दस्य सत्सप्तम्याश्च सहप्रयोगोऽपूर्वः ।

—:0:—

APPENDIX II.

—:o:—

(a). अत्र कश्चिदूहः — बाणसंज्ञः कविरेव बाणशब्दशक्याशुगप्रतिष्ठितशीघ्रगामित्वधर्मोपचारभङ्ग्या धावकशब्देन शीघ्रगामिवाचिना पुरा व्यपदिष्टः । तथा धावयति विद्रावयति प्रतिकवीन् इति, धावति काव्यनिर्माणसरणौ शीघ्रं गच्छतीति च व्युत्पत्त्या स धावको वक्तुमर्हः । तथाच प्रतिकविविद्रावकत्वं क्षिप्रकाव्यनिर्मातृत्वम् आशुगवाचकबाणशब्दबोध्यत्वमित्येतत्त्रितययोगिनं धर्मिणमेकं शक्तिलक्षणाभ्यां धावकशब्दः प्रतिपादयितुं समर्थ इति कृत्वा स बाणकवौ विदग्धैर्नूनं निवेशितः । न तु धावक इति बाणातिरिक्तः कश्चित् पुरुषविशेष आसीत् । एवं सति 'श्रीहर्षादेर्बाणादीनामिव धनम्' इति काश्मीरिकः पण्डितदुर्गाप्रसाददृष्टः काव्यप्रकाशपाठोऽपि 'धावकादीनामिव' इत्युपदर्शितपाठसमानार्थत्वात् स्वरसत उपपन्नो भवतीति ॥

(b). भासस्तुत्यर्थः कश्चिदयमर्थवादो लोकप्रसिद्ध उपन्यस्तः । 'विष्णुधर्मादहद्' इत्यत्र 'विष्णुधर्मान्' इतिच्छेदे भासव्यासकाव्ययोरुभयोरपि विष्णुधर्मप्रतिपादकानंशानाग्निर्न दग्धवानित्यर्थः । एवञ्चोभयोः साम्यं फलितम् । विष्णुधर्मादितिच्छेदे तथा मूलपाठकल्पने च पूर्ववदेवार्थः । किन्तु विष्णुधर्मानिति मूलपाठे प्रतिपाद्यप्रतिपादकयोरभेदोपचारेण विष्णुधर्माणां प्रतिपादकं भासस्य काव्यमित्यर्थो वक्तव्यः । स च क्लिष्टः सरसकाव्याननुगुणश्च । यदि तु मूले विष्णुधर्मानित्यत्र नकारस्य लेखकप्रमादायातत्वं कल्प्येत, तदा विष्णुधर्मशब्दः प्रथमैकवचनान्तः 'सः' इत्यस्य विशेषणम् । विष्णुर्व्यापकः सर्वत्र क्रमणशीलो धर्मो दाहकस्वरूपो यस्य स तथाभूत इति तदर्थः । औत्सर्गिकदाहस्वभाववानिति यावत् । तथाभूतोऽग्निरपि भासकाव्यं न ददाहेत्यग्निदिव्यपरीक्षोत्तीर्णे भासकाव्यप्राशस्त्यं प्रतिपादितं भवति । पूर्वोक्तपाठयोस्तु भगवद्धर्माणामग्निदिव्यपरीक्षोत्तीर्णत्वं प्रतिपादितं स्यात् । तच्च काव्यगुणप्रस्तावे न प्रकृतम् । किन्तु तृतीयपाठे व्याख्यानपद्धतिरनुकूलेव लक्ष्यते, तस्यां विष्णुधर्मानित्यंशे नकारत्यागस्य 'तयोर्मध्यात्' इति वाक्ये 'भासस्य काव्यम्' इत्यनयोः पदयोर्निवेशस्य च पूर्वोक्तार्थलाभाय कल्प्यत्वात् । सर्वथा श्लोकव्याख्ययोः पाठशुद्धिर्मातृकान्तरे परीक्षणीयैव ॥

(c). पुराणत्वात् सर्वं न साधु, किन्तु किञ्चिदसाध्वपि भवतीत्यर्थः । तथा नवत्वात् सर्वं नावद्यं, किञ्चित् किञ्चिद् अनवद्यमपि भवतीत्यर्थः ॥

(d). यास्तु मूलभाषायाः शाखा असंस्कृताः पूर्वमुक्ताः, ता अपि प्राकृतप-देन कामं व्यपदेष्टुं शक्याः, प्रकृतिरौत्पत्तिकं मूलभाषारूपं, तस्याः सम्बन्धि औत्पत्तिकमूलभाषारूपप्रचुरमित्यर्थाद्, असंस्कृतत्वसादृश्यनिमित्तादुपचाराद्वा ॥

(e). अस्य तिस्रः संज्ञाश्चाणक्यः कौटल्यो विष्णुगुप्त इति; यदाह कामन्द-कनीतिसारजयमङ्गला — "विष्णुगुप्त इति सांस्कारिकी संज्ञा, चाणक्यः कौटल्य इति तु जन्मभूमिगोत्रनिबन्धने" इति। विष्णुभक्तेन तत्पित्रा 'विष्णुरक्षित' इत्य-र्थकं विष्णुगुप्तनामधेयं कृतं स्याद्, बुद्धभक्तेन स्वपुत्रस्य बुद्धरक्षितनामेव। तेन चाणक्यब्राह्मणो विष्णुभक्तवंश्योऽपि विज्ञेयः ॥

(f). अविमारकनाटकाश्रितम् अविमारकचरितं भारतादिषु न दृश्यते। किन्तु तत्कथास्वभावपर्यालोचनायां कस्मिंश्चिदार्षेतिहासग्रन्थे तेन वर्णितेन भाव्य-मिति प्रतिभाति। स च भासकाले स्थितः पश्चाल्लुप्तश्च नूनम्। कामसूत्रव्याख्यायां जयमङ्गलायां पारदारिकाधिकरणे चतुर्थाध्याये अविमारकचरितमन्यथोक्तम्। यथा --

"तत्र सिद्धा द्वितीयेऽहनि वाचि वक्त्रे दृष्ट्यां च प्रसादमुपलक्ष्य पुनरपि कथां प्रवर्तयेत्। शृण्वत्यां चाहल्याविमारकशकुन्तलादीन्यन्यान्यपि लौकिकानि च कथयेत् तद्युक्तानि।" (वात्स्या० काम० पार० अ०४.)

इयमस्य व्याख्या जयमङ्गला —

"अग्निहोत्रके (ना?णा)ग्निपरिचरणे वधूर्नियुक्ता। सा च कुण्डादुत्थितेन मूर्तिमताग्निना कामिता। जातगर्भा च तां श्वशुरः कुलदोषभयादटव्यां तत्याज। प्रसूता च (सह सुतेन?? सुतम्। तं) शबरसेनापतिरपत्यबुद्ध्या संवर्धितवान्। तत्पुत्रश्चाजाविकसमूहेन बालवयस्त्वात् क्रीडमानः परिभ्रमन् क्षीरपानान्महाबलोऽभूत्। येन शिशुरेव हस्तग्रहणादजाविकं जघान। सेनापतिरप्यन्वर्थमस्य नाम चक्रेऽविमारक इति। ततः प्रवृद्धयौवनः कदाचिद् राज्ञोऽटव्यां समावासितस्य दुहितरं हस्तिना व्यापाद्यमानां तं हत्वा ररक्ष। ततो जातोत्कण्ठा सा स्वयमेव पाणिं ग्राहि-तवती।" इति। कथासरित्सागरे तु (११२. तरङ्गे.) अविमारकनामानुल्लेखेन कुरङ्गीचण्डालकथान्यथैव कथ्यते ॥